THE WILL KIT

JOHN VENTURA

 Dearborn
Financial Publishing, Inc.

Acquisitions Editor: Christine E. Litavsky
Managing Editor: Jack Kiburz
Project Editor: Karen A. Christensen
Cover Design: S. Laird Jenkins Corporation
Interior Design: Lucy Jenkins

© 1996 by John Ventura

Published by Dearborn Financial Publishing, Inc.®

Printed in the United States of America

96 97 98 10 9 8 7 6 5 4 3 2 1

Library of Congress Cataloging-in-Publication Data

Ventura, John
      The will kit / John Ventura.
          p.   cm.
      Includes index.
      ISBN 0-7931-1684-8
      1. Wills—United States—Popular works.   2. Estate planning—
United States—Popular works.   I. Title.
KF755.Z9V46   1996
346.7305′4—dc20
[347.30654]   96-13859
                                                                   CIP

Dearborn Financial Publishing books are available at special quantity discounts to use as premiums and sales promotions, or for use in corporate training programs. For more information, please call the Special Sales Manager at 800-621-9621, ext. 4384, or write to Dearborn Financial Publishing, Inc., 155 N. Wacker Drive, Chicago, IL 60606-1719.

Dedication

To my children, Stephanie, Erica and Colorado

Acknowledgments

My deepest appreciation to Mary Reed, who cares about this book as much as I do. Also, special thanks to estate attorney Jerry Frank Jones of Austin for his invaluable input.

Books by John Ventura

The Bankruptcy Kit

The Credit Repair Kit

Fresh Start!

The Small Business Survival Kit

The Will Kit

Contents

Preface

Most Americans die without having done estate planning of any kind, even something so simple as writing a legally valid will. I find their failure to plan what will happen to their money, home and other property after they die sadly ironic. Just think how hard most of us work all of our lives to buy a home, no matter how modest, lead a comfortable life and have something to pass on to our loved ones! Yet if we die without having done even the most basic estate planning, we have no guarantee that our hard-earned wealth will go to the people we would want to benefit from it.

Numerous reasons explain why so many Americans do so little estate planning. Some of us simply never get around to it because we're busy, because estate planning doesn't sound like fun or because we think that we have plenty of time to worry about planning our estates. Others mistakenly view estate planning as something that only rich people need to do. Finally, many people don't want to think about writing a will or doing any other estate planning because they feel uncomfortable confronting the reality of their own deaths.

I hope this book helps readers begin to appreciate that estate planning is something all adults with property should do if they want to be sure that when they die, their loved ones will be financially cared for and won't be saddled with legal and financial problems that could have been avoided. If writing a will is all the estate planning a reader does after finishing this book, I'll consider it to have been a success!

I also hope this book helps educate readers about the wide range of estate planning tools available to them. Most people limit their concept of estate planning to writing a will. In fact, estate planning is much more. For example, writing a living will that spells out the kind of medical care you want or don't want if you are dying is a part of estate planning.

I have two other, perhaps more unusual, goals for this book. First, I want to make the subject of estate planning as entertaining as possible. Therefore, throughout the book, I've included anecdotes about the estate planning some celebrities, successful businesspeople and other well-known individuals did or didn't do. They include people as diverse as Elvis Presley, Humphrey Bogart, President Dwight D. Eisenhower, Kurt Cobain, Jerry Garcia, Joan Crawford and the fabulously wealthy Doris Duke. Appendix A includes the actual wills of some of these people.

Second, I want to expand readers' definition of what they can include in their wills. Most of us tend to think of wills as dry, legal documents that spell out in legal terms what we want done with our property when we die. In fact, your will can be much more. It doesn't have to deal with only your money, home, stocks, mutual funds and other assets. It can be a very personal vehicle for conveying messages to your family and close friends. You can use your will to say final goodbyes to your loved ones or to convey special messages to special people. Perhaps you have something you have always wanted to say to someone but were unable to because you were shy, embarrassed or too emotional. Or perhaps you want to make sure that the important people in your life know just how important they are to you and why. You can include all of this in your will. No matter how much or little actual property you have to give to others, you can always give them a part of yourself by including personal messages of love and appreciation and other sentiments in your will. If you do, your will becomes much more than a dry, legal document, and writing one becomes a highly personal and meaningful experience.

An important note about this book: Although it provides detailed information about how to write a will and even includes sample wills and clauses, the text is not meant as a substitute for an attorney's help. It is intended to provide you with enough basic information about the subject of estate planning to make you feel comfortable meeting with an attorney and making informed decisions about your estate.

It's always advisable to get the advice of a qualified professional regarding the best way to legally transfer your property to others. Although for most people writing a will is all the estate planning they will need to do, an attorney can familiarize you with other kinds of estate planning you may want to consider. Also, an attorney can help you identify potential estate-related issues you may have overlooked that could cause problems later for your spouse or other beneficiaries. And best of all, the help of an attorney probably won't cost a lot.

Even if you are certain that you can write your own will, I advise you to hire an attorney to write the final version based on your draft. That way, you'll be assured that your will meets the legal standards of your state and that it will actually do what you want it to do.

I hope you learn from this book and enjoy it too!

CHAPTER
ONE

An Introduction to Estate Planning

This chapter will introduce you to estate planning. It will tell you exactly what estate planning is, as well as explain why it's important and who should do it. It will also identify a range of estate planning tools people of modest wealth may want to consider using; however, this chapter will focus on the cornerstone of estate planning—the will. (Subsequent chapters will discuss the other estate planning tools.) In this chapter, you will also learn about property laws, which affect what you can and can't give away.

What Is an Estate and What Is Estate Planning?

When you hear the word *estate,* you may envision something grandiose and far beyond your own financial reality. However, in the eyes of the law, your estate is simply everything you own, by yourself or with others. Your home, car, furniture, bank accounts, jewelry, life

Those of us who saw the movie *On Golden Pond* in 1981 witnessed a great actor, Henry Fonda, work with his daughter Jane and the wonderful Katharine Hepburn. In the movie, a retired old professor, played by Henry Fonda, and his wife, played by Hepburn, spend a summer at a lakeside cottage. Fonda, grouchy and hard to get along with, learns through his grandson how to be a father. This comes a little late for his grown daughter, played by Jane Fonda, who has spent her life feeling that her father never really cared much about her.

On January 22, 1981, the same year that *On Golden Pond* came out, Henry Fonda signed his last will. It was only three pages long, but it expressed in a simple and direct way a thoughtful consideration for his family.

A year later, Henry Fonda died, leaving a legacy of great film roles. On the silver screen, he was always at his best when he played a humble man faced with big problems. When you read his will in Appendix A, you can see how much he was a simple man in real life, too. For example, he provides modest instructions concerning his funeral and cremation: "It is my wish that there be no funeral or memorial service at the time of my death, and that my remains be promptly cremated and disposed of without ceremony of any kind."

insurance policy, retirement plan, stocks and bonds, and other assets are all part of your estate. Although some people have large estates worth millions, the estates of most Americans are relatively modest.

Regardless of the size of your estate, if you care about what will happen to your property after you die, you must plan your estate while you live. The exact planning you do depends on the value and complexity of your estate and your estate planning goals. Subsequent chapters of this book will give you an overview of your basic estate planning options.

Proper estate planning allows you to accomplish the following four key goals:

1. *Ensure that when you die, your property will legally transfer to your spouse, to your children or to whomever you wish.*

The people who receive your property are called your *beneficiaries.* You get to play Santa Claus!

2. *Protect your estate from the claims of any creditors you may owe money to at the time of your death.* Doing so means that more of what you own will go to your beneficiaries.

3. *Minimize any taxes your estate may owe after you die, leaving more for your beneficiaries.* Tax minimization is typically a concern only for people with substantial estates.

4. *Plan for the possibility that when you are old, you may become unable to make decisions for yourself due to physical or mental incapacitation.* Through estate planning, you can establish legal mechanisms to manage your personal and business finances and to direct your health care. In fact, anyone with property, not just senior citizens, should have such legal mechanisms in place because even those who are not old can be incapacitated by an illness or an accident and become unable to manage their own affairs. These mechanisms can help prevent your estate from being depleted by the cost of medical care you might not want if you could speak for yourself; ensure the continued integrity of your personal and business affairs; and spare your family from having to make potentially difficult and emotionally painful decisions regarding your personal affairs and medical care.

Planning your estate also will bring you peace of mind. It is a good feeling knowing that you have planned for your own death, that you have provided as best you can for your family and that you have done what you can to ensure that your loved ones won't face the legal and financial problems that can result if you didn't do such planning. Estate planning is the ultimate act of love.

To help you further understand exactly what estate planning can do for you and why it's important, Figure 1.1 provides a list of specific things estate planning can accomplish. Each of them will be addressed in subsequent chapters of this book.

According to *Classic Cases: The Estates of Famous Americans* (Dearborn Financial Publishing, Inc., 1990), Henry Fonda had a gross estate of $4,339,788 and a net estate of $4,306,743. (See Figure 1.2.) He appears to have planned his estate well, given how little it paid in settlement costs—debts, attorney and executor fees and taxes—after

FIGURE 1.1

---

11 Things Estate Planning Can Accomplish

1. Provide financially for your spouse, dependent children and others after you die. Financial planning is something you do to build your wealth; estate planning is something you do to help ensure that this wealth goes to the people you want to benefit from it.

2. Arrange for the care and financial well-being of your minor children in the event both you and your spouse die.

3. Legally transfer your property to your beneficiaries.

4. Control, even after your death, how and when your beneficiaries will take complete possession of the money and other property you leave them.

5. Ensure that the maximum amount of your estate goes to your beneficiaries rather than toward paying probate costs, legal and executor fees and other expenses.

6. Minimize the taxes your estate may be liable to pay and arrange for their payment. Estate-related taxes are usually a concern only for people with substantial estates.

7. Minimize cost and delays in the distribution of your estate to your beneficiaries.

8. Minimize potential creditor claims to your estate when you die and fund those your estate will have to pay.

9. Plan for the future of your business if you become incapacitated or die.

10. Arrange for the management of your finances and medical care in the event you're unable to do so for yourself due to physical or mental illness or incapacitation.

11. Plan and fund your funeral and burial or your cremation.

FIGURE 1.2

Henry Fonda: Net Estate Table
Prominent Actor, Los Angeles, California

GROSS ESTATE **$4,339,788**

Debts   *$3,545*
Attorney Fees   *29,500*
Executor Fees   *Waived*
Fed. Estate Tax* ($2,080,183)   *None*

TOTAL COSTS **$33,045**

NET ESTATE **$4,306,743**

*Full marital deduction (Estimated estate tax without marital deduction)

he died. On the other hand, the estate of Elvis Presley did not fare so well. (See Figure 1.3.) Although his gross estate was considerably larger than Fonda's, settlement costs ate up approximately 73 percent of it, leaving his beneficiaries with less than Fonda's received! You will find Presley's will in Appendix A.

Estate Planning Tools

A legally valid will is the cornerstone of most estate plans; however, it is only one of many estate planning tools you can use. Other tools include but are not limited to

- joint ownership;
- life insurance;
- retirement plans;
- gifts you make while alive—*inter vivos* gifts;
- payable-on-death and trust accounts;
- testamentary trusts;
- living trusts;

FIGURE 1.3

Elvis Presley: Net Estate Table
Superstar of Rock and Roll, Memphis, Tennessee

GROSS ESTATE* **$10,165,434**

Debts	*$3,832,552*
Administrative Expenses	*114,563*
Attorney Fees	*18,000*
Executor Fees	*70,000*
Tenn. Inheritance Tax	*526,435*
Calif. Inheritance Tax	*27,500*
*Fed. Estate Tax***	*2,785,585*

TOTAL COSTS **$7,374,635**

CASH IN ESTATE **$1,933,759**

NET ESTATE **$2,790,799**

---

*Press accounts reported the Presley estate to be worth as much as $15 million because gross assets in the testamentary trust rose to this figure in the year after the singer's death, when $4,672,710 in royalties and other income went into the trust during this period. Included in the gross estate is $63,660 of life insurance.

**No marital deduction

- living wills;
- powers of attorney, including a durable health care power of attorney; and
- burial instructions.

The right tools for you depend on, among other things, your estate planning goals, the size and complexity of your estate, your marital status and age, whether you have any minor children and the needs of your beneficiaries. Over the years, as your wealth increases and as the needs and circumstances of you and your family change, your estate planning needs will change, too, and new tools may become appropriate. In fact, you should periodically review your estate plan.

What Is a Will and Why Is It Important?

A will is your legal voice after death. For Henry Fonda, it was a chance to say that although he cared for his children Peter and Jane, they did not need his wealth, and therefore he would leave it to his wife, Shirlee, and his other daughter, Amy, because they depended on him for financial support.

Writing a will provides you with the opportunity to spell out what you want done with certain types of property after you die and to name the executor of your estate. This person will be in charge of your estate after you die and will be responsible for carrying out a number of duties. You can read more about executors in Chapter 3.

A will is not just for rich people, for senior citizens or for people of a certain age. It is something that anyone with assets should prepare. Depending on your situation, a will may be the only estate planning tool you need. However, even if you use other tools, you should always have an up-to-date and legally valid will.

If you have a minor child, a will is even more important. Depending on your state, it may be the only way you can legally designate a personal guardian for your minor child. This person would raise your child if both you and your spouse die.

What Happens When You Die Without a Will?

Rock star Kurt Cobain took his own life in 1994. It was sad to see this bright new musician mourned by his legions of fans. After his death, it was determined that he did not have a will to provide for his wife, Courtney Love-Cobain, or their daughter, Frances B. Cobain. A copy of the petition for Letter of Administration reveals that this young man's success had generated an estate that would exceed $1.2 million. (See Appendix A.)

Understanding what can happen if you die without a will—that is, *intestate*—should help underscore the importance of having one.

Nothing may happen at first. No official will knock at your spouse's door or send your family a letter informing them of the problems and expenses they may now face because you didn't write a will. However, trouble could develop later if, for example, your family or another person close to you, like your unmarried partner, wants to sell or borrow against one of your assets after you die. Let's assume that your wife decides she wants to sell the home both of you lived in so she can move into a smaller place. If, as part of your estate planning, you didn't arrange for her to have full legal ownership of the house after you die, she'll have to initiate a legal process to get full ownership before she can sell the property.

If you die without a will, a series of consequences will be triggered. First, unless one of your legal heirs—a relative who is legally in line to inherit from you—comes forward to act as the *administrator* of your estate (the person who performs the duties of an executor), your local probate judge may appoint an administrator to perform the duties your executor would have performed had you named one in your will. That person may or may not be someone familiar to and trusted by your family. The administrator is entitled to receive a fee for carrying out the duties of the job. Your estate will pay that fee, leaving less for your heirs.

Second, the probate judge, not you, will decide who inherits your assets. To make that determination, the court will try to identify and locate your legal heirs and will distribute your property among them, according to the laws of your state. This can mean that the assets you own will go to people you would prefer didn't receive them and that your spouse may not get all of the assets you had expected he or she would inherit after your death. For example, your property may end up being split between your spouse and your children, possibly meaning that your spouse doesn't have enough to meet his or her financial needs or that each of your children will receive the same share of your estate even though they may be in very different financial circumstances. The state may even give some of your property to family members you don't like or don't even know! Also, because the probate judge will distribute your assets only to your legal heirs, none of your estate will go to your special friends or favorite charities.

Let's go back to Henry Fonda's will to illustrate what can happen if the probate court gets involved in the disposition of someone's assets. We know from Fonda's will that he wanted his estate to go to his wife Shirlee and to his daughter Amy, not to his daughter Jane and son Peter. However, if he had died without a will, the laws of California would have distributed his property to his legal heirs, which would have meant that Jane, Peter, Shirlee, Amy and possibly other relatives would each have received a share of his estate.

In many states, a will is the only legal vehicle a parent can use to name a personal guardian for a minor child—in most states, that means a child younger than age 18. Failing to designate a guardian for your minor child should that child be left parentless can have devastating consequences. First, if no relatives or close friends come forward to raise your child, the court will determine who will have that responsibility. This could mean that your child might be raised by a relative you don't like or respect or even by someone you don't know if no relatives are available to help. Second, if an adult raises your child without the legal designation of "personal guardian," problems could develop. For example, the caretaker might be prevented from adding your child to his or her medical plan; might be unable to register your child for school; or might have no right to grant consent for the child to receive certain types of medical care. Therefore, your child's unofficial guardian will have to initiate a court process to be named legal guardian.

Writing a will also gives you the opportunity to name a *property guardian* for your young child. This person would manage the property you leave your child in your will, assuming its value exceeds the maximum each state says a minor may own without the active involvement of an adult. Therefore, if you don't write a will and your minor child inherits property valued at more than your state's maxi-

 HOT TIP

If your minor child is the beneficiary of your life insurance policy or annuity, the funds will not be released until a property guardian or another adult with legal authority to manage those funds has been appointed.

mum, the court will have to appoint someone to manage your child's inheritance until he or she becomes a legal adult, age 18 in most states.

If you die without a will, a close relative or friend, perhaps the person who acts as personal guardian for your child, will have to initiate the probate of your estate and ask to be named property guardian. This person may not be someone you trust or someone who might not have good money management skills. Yet once named property guardian, that person will gain access to a portion of your estate so that he or she can use the resources to help pay for your child's care and education. If no one comes forward and the court can't find anyone qualified within your family to assume this role, it will appoint a professional property guardian to manage your child's estate and to disburse income as necessary to your child's personal guardian. A professional charges a substantial amount of money every year for acting as property guardian. That sum will be deducted from your child's estate.

Dying without a will can have other consequences, too. First, especially if your estate is substantial or if bad blood already runs among your heirs, they may fight among themselves about who gets what. Although interfamily conflict is possible even with a will, having one should help minimize the potential for trouble after you die.

Second, without a will, your estate will probably incur fees and expenses it wouldn't otherwise. Because your estate will pay those fees and expenses, less will remain for your heirs.

Get Legal Help

Theoretically, if your estate is relatively modest, your family situation not complex and your estate planning goals straightforward, you can prepare your own simple will—a will that does not include a testamentary trust. However, this is usually not a good idea, and hiring an attorney is strongly recommended for a number of important reasons (see Figure 1.4):

- If your will doesn't meet certain legal standards and if your wishes and intentions are not worded correctly, the document will not be legally valid or may not achieve your estate planning goals. In fact, a poorly written will can trigger the same negative consequences as can dying *intestate*.

FIGURE 1.4

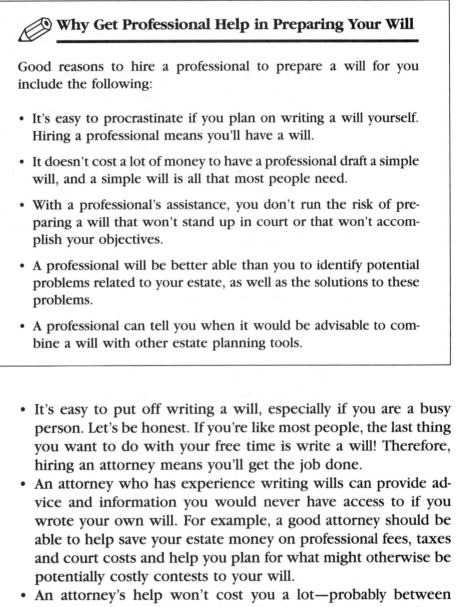

✏️ **Why Get Professional Help in Preparing Your Will**

Good reasons to hire a professional to prepare a will for you include the following:

- It's easy to procrastinate if you plan on writing a will yourself. Hiring a professional means you'll have a will.

- It doesn't cost a lot of money to have a professional draft a simple will, and a simple will is all that most people need.

- With a professional's assistance, you don't run the risk of preparing a will that won't stand up in court or that won't accomplish your objectives.

- A professional will be better able than you to identify potential problems related to your estate, as well as the solutions to these problems.

- A professional can tell you when it would be advisable to combine a will with other estate planning tools.

- It's easy to put off writing a will, especially if you are a busy person. Let's be honest. If you're like most people, the last thing you want to do with your free time is write a will! Therefore, hiring an attorney means you'll get the job done.
- An attorney who has experience writing wills can provide advice and information you would never have access to if you wrote your own will. For example, a good attorney should be able to help save your estate money on professional fees, taxes and court costs and help you plan for what might otherwise be potentially costly contests to your will.
- An attorney's help won't cost you a lot—probably between $500 and $1,000. Exactly how much you'll pay depends on where you live, the size and complexity of your estate, whether you expect any contests to your will or creditor problems after you die, the kind of tax planning you may have to do and

whether you hire an attorney who is a general practitioner or one who specializes in estate planning. For $1,000, many estate attorneys will provide you with a will that includes a testamentary trust as well as a durable power of attorney and a living will.

- If you own a business, an attorney can advise you about the special estate planning issues you need to address, such as business succession and liquidity.
- An attorney can point out issues or potential problems you might not be aware of. For example, if you're like a growing number of people who have been married before and have children from a previous marriage, an attorney can advise you about how to ensure that those children receive a share of your property when you or your current spouse dies. Without that advice, if you leave all of your property to your current spouse, your children could end up with nothing.
- An attorney can explain probate to you and help you plan for it. Probate is a legal process that, among other things, affects the transfer of the property in your will to your designated beneficiaries.

HOT TIP

Be sure that the attorney you hire is someone you feel comfortable with because you'll have to share with him or her personal information about yourself and your family.

Even if your estate is small, don't assume that you need no help from an attorney. You do. In fact, you may need an attorney's help more than someone with a substantial estate! Because you have less to leave your beneficiaries, it's important that you do everything you can to make sure that as much of your wealth as possible goes to them. For example, if your estate is worth $90,000 and you make a mistake in your estate planning that costs your estate $10,000 after you die, your estate will be reduced by 11 percent. But if your estate is worth $900,000, a $10,000 mistake will reduce your estate by only 1 percent!

To locate a qualified attorney, get a reference from a friend, a family member, your CPA or your financial adviser; contact your local or state bar; or write to the American College of Trust and Estate Counsel (3415 South Sepulveda Boulevard, Suite 330, Los Angeles, CA 90034). Other referral sources include your doctor, your dentist or a successful businessperson you know. All are likely to have substantial estates and have probably done some estate planning with the help of an attorney.

What Is a Modest Estate?

Several times, this chapter has used the term *modest estate.* Let's define what that means. From the law's perspective, a modest estate is considered to be one worth less than $600,000. For some of you, a car, furniture and some personal items may represent your entire estate, the value of which may not be close to $600,000. However, many of you, especially if you're a homeowner and have accumulated other assets like life insurance, retirement benefits and stocks and bonds, may be surprised to discover just how much your estate is actually worth.

People with modest estates do not have to worry about how much Uncle Sam will take from their estates in federal estate taxes when they die. That is a concern for people with estates valued at more than $600,000. However, even modest estates may have to pay state estate taxes.

If You Decide To Prepare Your Own Simple Will

If, despite this book's advice, you decide to prepare your own simple will, before you begin, take time to understand federal tax laws related to wills and property as well as the applicable laws of your state. Otherwise, your will may not be valid or it may not accomplish your goals. This book will provide you with an overview of federal law. However, be aware that federal laws can change, so by the time you sit down to write your will, some of the information in this book may no longer be up to date. This is true of all books written for the public that contain legal information.

To get the specifics on the laws in your state, contact your state or county bar association or an attorney. If you have a law school in your area, you may also be able to get the information from a professor who teaches estate law.

When you write your will, use simple, precise language that leaves nothing to interpretation. Otherwise, your wishes may be misunderstood or your will may be vulnerable to contests from those omitted from it or those who are unhappy with what they or someone else received.

Types of Wills

A typed will, prepared in accordance with the rules of your state and written to reflect your own particular needs and concerns, is almost always best. However, other kinds of wills exist. Some have serious limitations or may not be recognized as legally valid in your state. So read the following sections with care.

Preprinted fill-in-the-blanks or *statutory* will. This includes the will generated by computer software you can now buy to help you create your own document. Although fill-in-the-blanks wills are legally valid in some states, they're not appropriate for many people because they cannot be customized to meet specific estate planning needs or concerns. However, if your estate is very small and simple and your family situation and estate planning goals are uncomplicated, a fill-in-the-blanks will may be all you need. Even so, before using this kind of will, it's a good idea to consult an estate planning attorney to make certain that the form you plan to use is legal in your state and to assure yourself that the document will truly meet your needs.

Handwritten or *holographic* will. This kind of will is recognized as legal by some states under certain conditions. When a question exists about the validity and wording of a will, many courts apply less stringent requirements to a handwritten will than to a typed will; in fact, they may "lean over backward" to accept it, assuming a court is confident that the handwriting is the willmaker's. One reason for the leniency is that because the will is handwritten, it's an especially personal document; also a handwritten will is harder to alter than a typed one, assuming it is written in pen not pencil.

Oral or *nuncupative* will. Very few states recognize this kind of will. Those states that do, recognize oral wills only in very specific circumstances, usually when a person is near death, has no written will and has no time to write one. States that recognize oral wills often require that a will's provisions be committed to writing soon after they are stated and limit the total value or type of the property that can be distributed by such a will.

Video will. This is a video of someone stating or reading the provisions of his or her will. Presently, no state recognizes video wills. However, if you're concerned about possible challenges to your written will based on allegations that you were not of sound mind when it was prepared, an additional video will might help prove otherwise. You might also want to videotape the execution of your written will as a defense against possible challenges.

Married Couples

If you're married, both you and your spouse should have separate wills. It is not advisable to share a single or joint will, even if you and your spouse own most of your property as joint tenants with right of survivorship or as tenants by the entirety. Usually, a joint will leaves all of a couple's assets to the surviving partner and also provides for the disposition of the assets after the survivor dies.

A key problem with a joint will is that your state may view it essentially as a contract between you and your spouse. If it does, the surviving spouse will not be able to change or revoke the will to respond to changes in his or her life or in the lives of your beneficiaries.

It's not necessary that your will and your spouse's will complement and reinforce one another. For example, each will can use a different asset disposal scheme. However, it is advisable for both of you to discuss your individual estate planning goals and needs before meeting with your attorney so there are no surprises.

Information Your Attorney Will Need

Prior to drafting your will, your attorney will want to meet with you at least once. The meeting will help your attorney begin gathering the information he or she needs to write a will that meets your objectives. See Figure 1.5 for a list of the information your attorney will request.

If you or your spouse owns or has an interest in a small or closely held business, your attorney will also want to see the following, where applicable: partnership agreement, shareholders' agreement, limited liability company operation agreement, articles of incorporation, corporate bylaws, tax returns, buy-sell agreements and other necessary documents.

What Makes a Will Legally Valid?

The characteristics of a legally valid will vary from state to state. However, ten general characteristics are summarized in Figure 1.6.

Other Characteristics

No will is exactly the same because no one owns exactly the same assets, has the same beneficiaries and shares the same estate planning goals. However, most wills include similar types of information, including

- a clause invalidating all previous wills you may have written;
- the names of your estate executor and substitute executor;
- the names of your beneficiaries and substitute beneficiaries or the classes of your beneficiaries (for example, "all of my children") and exactly what property you leave to each;
- directions regarding how any estate-related expenses, including debts and taxes, should be paid; and
- a clause that leaves to a residuary beneficiary anything that may be left in your estate after all other property has been distributed to specific beneficiaries and after all estate taxes, fees and other expenses have been paid.

FIGURE 1.5

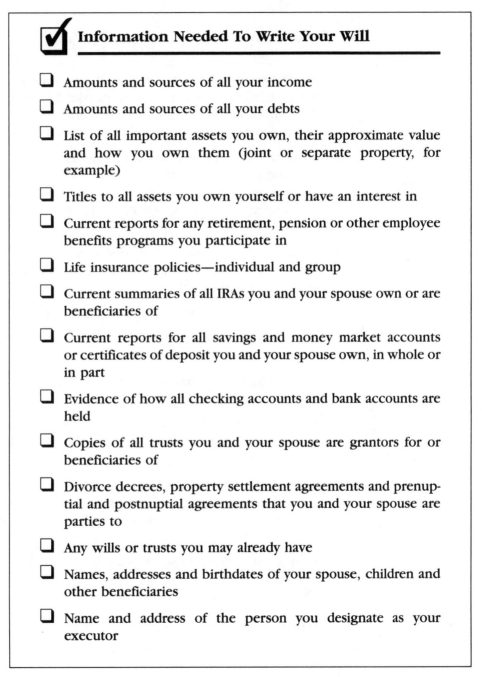

☑ Information Needed To Write Your Will

❏ Amounts and sources of all your income

❏ Amounts and sources of all your debts

❏ List of all important assets you own, their approximate value and how you own them (joint or separate property, for example)

❏ Titles to all assets you own yourself or have an interest in

❏ Current reports for any retirement, pension or other employee benefits programs you participate in

❏ Life insurance policies—individual and group

❏ Current summaries of all IRAs you and your spouse own or are beneficiaries of

❏ Current reports for all savings and money market accounts or certificates of deposit you and your spouse own, in whole or in part

❏ Evidence of how all checking accounts and bank accounts are held

❏ Copies of all trusts you and your spouse are grantors for or beneficiaries of

❏ Divorce decrees, property settlement agreements and prenuptial and postnuptial agreements that you and your spouse are parties to

❏ Any wills or trusts you may already have

❏ Names, addresses and birthdates of your spouse, children and other beneficiaries

❏ Name and address of the person you designate as your executor

FIGURE 1.6

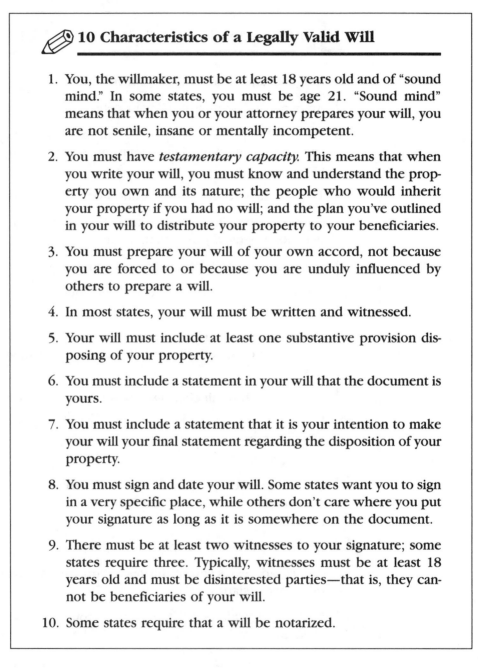

10 Characteristics of a Legally Valid Will

1. You, the willmaker, must be at least 18 years old and of "sound mind." In some states, you must be age 21. "Sound mind" means that when you or your attorney prepares your will, you are not senile, insane or mentally incompetent.

2. You must have *testamentary capacity.* This means that when you write your will, you must know and understand the property you own and its nature; the people who would inherit your property if you had no will; and the plan you've outlined in your will to distribute your property to your beneficiaries.

3. You must prepare your will of your own accord, not because you are forced to or because you are unduly influenced by others to prepare a will.

4. In most states, your will must be written and witnessed.

5. Your will must include at least one substantive provision disposing of your property.

6. You must include a statement in your will that the document is yours.

7. You must include a statement that it is your intention to make your will your final statement regarding the disposition of your property.

8. You must sign and date your will. Some states want you to sign in a very specific place, while others don't care where you put your signature as long as it is somewhere on the document.

9. There must be at least two witnesses to your signature; some states require three. Typically, witnesses must be at least 18 years old and must be disinterested parties—that is, they cannot be beneficiaries of your will.

10. Some states require that a will be notarized.

Legal Restrictions

No matter what state you live in, you cannot do certain things in your will. First, you may not give away property you don't own. Also, you may not give a gift to a beneficiary to force or encourage that person to take an action or behave in a manner that your state does not consider to be in the interest of good public policy. For example, your state would probably view a stipulation in your will that your son can receive certain property only if he divorces his wife as being not in the interest of good public policy because the state would not want to promote divorce.

In no state may you leave money to a beneficiary for an illegal purpose. And, finally, you may not require that your executor use a specific attorney.

Some states also restrict charitable gift giving through a will. These states include Florida, Georgia, Idaho, Mississippi, Montana and Ohio; the District of Columbia follows suit.

Where To Keep Your Will

Store your will in a secure and accessible location, and let your executor and at least one close family member know where it is. Storage options include a safe-deposit box at your bank, a file at your attorney's office or a fireproof safe at your home. However, before storing your will in a safe-deposit box, find out whether your state restricts access to it after you die. Many states require that a safe-deposit box be sealed upon the owner's death and opened only after certain conditions are met. Complying with such a restriction could delay initiation of the probate process.

Before you store your will, it's a good idea to give a copy of it to your executor. You may also want to give a copy to your spouse or primary beneficiary unless you have some reason you do not want others to know what your will contains. If you do give your will to others, be sure that everyone gets a copy of any changes, or *codicils,* you may add. If you revoke your will, get all copies of the old will back or make sure they are destroyed. Otherwise, confusion may arise after you die as to which version of your will is valid. That confusion could delay probate and the distribution of your estate to your beneficiaries. Unsigned copies of your will can also cause confusion.

HOT TIP

Don't make any duplicate originals of your will.

Wills and Single People

If you're young and single, you probably own little property; therefore, a simple will is likely all the estate planning you need. However, as you age and your wealth grows, you may want to explore other estate planning tools.

Liberace, a famous pianist, was the most spectacularly flamboyant entertainer of his time during the early days of Las Vegas and television. Before he died unmarried in 1987, he created the Liberace Revocable Trust, which ensured that his estate would go to the individuals and organizations he most cared for. He describes this trust in his will, included in Appendix A.

If you live with someone in a committed, unmarried relationship and want to be sure that when you die, your partner receives all or a significant share of your estate, include that person in your will. You may also want to name him or her as the beneficiary of your life insurance policy and any employee benefits or retirement plans you may have. Additional estate planning tools may also be appropriate depending on your circumstances.

Estate planning is especially important for lesbian and gay couples because inheritance laws do not recognize their relationships and because judges may not view their partnerships with favor should no will exist. Therefore, same-sex couples should get legal help when drafting their wills or any other estate-related documents so that their intentions and desires are clearly spelled out and so that nothing is left to interpretation. This is especially important if a couple's family disapproves of the relationship or isn't aware of it. A gay or lesbian person may also want to name his or her partner as beneficiary of any insurance policies, retirement accounts and annuities and to give that partner a durable power of attorney.

HOT TIP

If you leave property to your unmarried partner rather than to certain relatives who, by law, would inherit—your heirs—clearly indicate in your will that you choose not to give anything to those family members. Explicitly disinheriting them helps discourage will contests by disgruntled relatives.

Wills and Divorce

Generally, if you get divorced, either your entire will or just those parts of it that relate to your former spouse are revoked automatically. Therefore, before you divorce, find out how this will affect your will and, if necessary, prepare a new will immediately.

What You Can and Can't Give Away with a Will

You can convey only some of the assets in your estate to your beneficiaries through a will. Those assets are described as "passing under" a will or as being "controlled by" a will. They include assets you and another person co-own as tenants in common (to be explained in a later section of this chapter), assets you own by yourself and that you control 100 percent.

When you die, only these assets will go through *probate,* a legal process that transfers your property to your beneficiaries. Collectively, those assets are called your *probate estate.*

Property that you cannot convey to your beneficiaries through your will is described as "passing over" or "outside" your will. When you die, this property will automatically transfer to your beneficiaries via some legal mechanism and do not go through probate. Property not controlled by a will includes the following:

- Property you and someone else own together as joint tenants with right of survivorship or that you and your spouse own together as tenants by the entirety (to be explained in a later section of this chapter)
- Life insurance proceeds. The person named in your policy as your beneficiary automatically receives the proceeds of the policy when you die. Even if your will leaves the proceeds to someone else, at your death, they go to your policy beneficiary.

 **HOT TIP**

If you name your estate as beneficiary of your life insurance policy, the policy proceeds will pass *under* rather than *over* your will, will go through probate and will be subject to the claims of your creditors.

- Proceeds from any retirement plans, pensions and IRAs you own that are payable to a beneficiary
- Totten trust and payable-on-death accounts
- *Inter vivos* gifts—gifts you make to others while you are still alive
- Assets placed in a living trust
- Partnerships. If you are in a partnership, your partnership agreement may limit your ability to transfer your interest to a beneficiary through your will. Other property controlled by a contract may present similar limitations.
- Personal property. In most cases, you can transfer the usual items of personal property with a written agreement rather than a will. However, this method of transfer is not legally binding, so your heirs could object.
- Your spouse's share of the community property you own together

FIGURE 1.7

Orville Wright: Net Estate Table
Aviation Pioneer, Dayton, Ohio

GROSS ESTATE **$1,023,904**

Debts	*$3,623*
Administrative Expenses	*16,656*
Attorney Fees	*20,360*
Executor Fees	*19,360*
Ohio Inheritance Tax	*26,673*
Fed. Estate Tax*	*164,971*

TOTAL COSTS **$251,643**

CASH IN ESTATE **$83,313**

NET ESTATE **$772,261**

*No marital deduction; no surviving spouse

 **HOT TIP**

If you live in a community property state and you leave your share of community property to your spouse in your will, that property may not have to go through probate. It depends on the laws of your state.

Understanding Property Law

When you think about your estate and which asset you want to leave to which beneficiary, it's important to have a basic understanding of property law because it affects what you can give away and how you can give it away. Although your attorney will explain some of this to you, property law can be confusing. The next sections of this chapter will provide you with a general overview of the law.

Ways To Own Property

How you own an asset affects your ability to give it to someone else. Therefore, when you acquire an asset, one of your considerations should always be how best to own it, especially if you are married or live in a committed but unmarried relationship. Check your deeds, titles, vehicle registration and other ownership documents to determine how you own your assets. If you are confused, talk with your attorney.

Joint Ownership

If you and another person share ownership of an asset, you own it jointly. Four types of joint ownership exist: joint tenancy with right of survivorship, tenancy in common, tenancy by the entirety and community property.

Joint tenancy with right of survivorship. With this type of ownership, your share of an asset automatically goes to the owner who survives you. Therefore, you cannot give away your share in your will or by using another estate planning tool. Joint tenancy can be a good way for married couples and unmarried couples in committed relationships to own property together. Bank accounts are often owned this way.

For example, Humphrey Bogart and his wife, Lauren Bacall Bogart, owned their home as joint tenants; therefore, it was not subject to disposition by will.

Tenancy by the entirety. Similar to joint tenancy with right of survivorship, only a husband and wife can own an asset this way. When one spouse dies, the other automatically owns the entire asset. This means you do not have to include it in your will, and you cannot use your will or any other estate planning tool to give it to someone else because it belongs to your spouse. About half of all states recognize this form of ownership, and some recognize it only as an ownership option for certain types of assets, often real estate.

Tenancy in common. If you own an asset as a *tenant in common,* you are part owner and your co-owners have no interest in your share. This means you are free to leave your share to whomever you want. It can be a good form of joint ownership for couples who want to purchase an asset together but who are unsure about the long-term future of their relationship.

Community property. This type of joint ownership applies only in certain states. It will be discussed in the following section.

Marital Property Laws

It is also important to have a basic understanding of marital property law because the type of marital property law recognized by your state affects what is yours to give away. It also affects the rights of your surviving spouse.

In the United States, two basic types of marital property law exist: community property law and common or separate property law. Most states are separate property states, but nine are community property states: Arizona, California, Idaho, Louisiana, Nevada, New Mexico, Texas, Washington and Wisconsin.

Community Property States

If you live in a community property state, you and your spouse each owns half of whatever property you acquire or income you earn during your marriage, regardless of whose name is on the ownership papers. Generally, if you move out of a community property state to a separate property state, the property and income you acquired while you lived in the first state remain community property. Property you owned and income you earned prior to your marriage are yours alone after you marry.

Exceptions to these rules exist, however. For example, if you receive a gift or an inheritance of any size while you are married, legally that property is not community property. However, if you deposit your inheritance in an account you share with your spouse or if you blend community and noncommunity property in some other way, separate property can effectively become community property. If this is of concern to you, talk with your attorney.

 **HOT TIP**

You and your spouse can draw up a prenuptial or post-nuptial agreement to exempt certain property you acquire or certain income you earn during your marriage from the marital property laws of your state. Such agreements should be done only with the assistance of an attorney who has experience preparing such contracts.

In some community property states, community property does not have the right of survivorship. That is, if you live in a community property state when you die, your surviving spouse will not automatically inherit your half of the community property. Instead, you must use estate planning to legally transfer it to your spouse. And you cannot give away your spouse's half unless he or she agrees to it. This helps protect your spouse from disinheritance. If you die without having conveyed your half of the community property to your spouse in your will or through some other legal mechanism, he or she will probably receive it anyway unless children are involved; then your spouse and your children could become co-owners of the property. If your spouse and children do not get along, this arrangement could create problems for everyone. Therefore, be sure not to overlook community property when you do your estate planning.

Separate Property States

If you are married and live in a separate property state, when you earn money, it is yours only; and when you purchase an asset with your own money, you own it 100 percent and your spouse has no interest in it. If you both contribute money to buy an asset, legally you both own it, assuming each of your names is on the title, deed and other documentation. However, if only your name appears on the ownership papers, you are the legal owner, not both you and your spouse. For example, assume that you and your spouse pool your money for a down payment on a new car and both of you contribute to the monthly payments. Despite the fact that both of you pay for the car, if only your name appears on the title, you, not you and your spouse, are its legal owner.

Community property can be changed into separate property. For example, you could give your community property to your spouse as a gift. To be certain that it is recognized as separate property, make the gift in writing.

 **HOT TIP**

Consult with an attorney before changing the nature of an asset from community property to separate property or vice versa.

CHAPTER
TWO

Completing an Estate Planning Worksheet

Taking inventory of all your assets and liabilities is an essential first step in estate planning and will preparation. You must compile this information for your attorney so he or she can understand the size and complexity of your estate and advise you about the estate planning you should do. Even if all you do is write a will, the inventory is information you need.

To help you organize your asset and liability information, this chapter provides a worksheet and will help you fill it out. After you complete the worksheet, you'll have not only a comprehensive list of your assets and liabilities but an estimate of your estate's net worth as well. The estimate will tell you and your attorney whether your estate planning should include estate tax minimization.

Dwight David Eisenhower, the American general who led the United States to victory in World War II and later became president, was born in 1890 and died 79 years later in 1969. The amount of assets he accumulated over many years of public and private life must have been staggering (see Figure 2.1). Yet as most presidents, he faced the task of providing for his family as well as determining how the memorabilia, writings and all else accumulated over a full life were to be disbursed.

Most presidents must anticipate that the United States would want some of their documents and effects to preserve the history and institution of the presidency.

In his will, former President Eisenhower gave to the United States for deposit in the Eisenhower Presidential Library in Abilene, Kansas, "all of my papers and other documentary materials, including books, still pictures, motion pictures and sound recordings." He also gave many other assets to the Eisenhower Foundation after he took care of his wife.

Few of us will ever have the problem of inventorying assets on such a grand scale for estate planning purposes as did President Eisenhower. Taking an inventory of assets will be a lot easier for most of us. In fact, some of us may think we own so little that completing an estate planning worksheet would be a waste of time. However, once you fill one out, you may be surprised to discover just how much you have to leave to others.

Determining What You Own

It's now time to take that first step in estate planning—listing and categorizing your assets. Use the examples and the worksheet provided in Figures 2.2 and 2.3. If you have trouble, ask your attorney for help.

You will notice that the worksheet includes spaces for listing and describing each of your assets and for indicating how you own each asset, the percentage of each asset you own and the estimated net value of each asset. Recording this information will help you identify two things: the assets you own and can transfer to your beneficiaries

FIGURE 2.1

Dwight D. Eisenhower: Net Estate Table
U.S. President, Five-Star General, U.S. Army, Author and
Statesman, Gettysburg, Pennsylvania

GROSS ESTATE $2,905,857

Debts	*$140,036*
Administrative Expenses	*21,853**
Attorney Fees	*68,900*
Executor Fees	*30,500*
Pa. Inheritance Tax	*42,026*
*Fed. Estate Tax***	*368,114*

TOTAL COSTS $671,429

CASH IN ESTATE $60,820

NET ESTATE $2,234,428

*Includes more than $6,500 to run farm until crops are harvested and sold.

**$1,145,118 marital deduction. Widow has life estate from trust funds.

and how much of your estate will go through probate. The latter can
help you determine the importance of minimizing, through your estate
planning, the number of assets that will go through probate or pursu-
ing eligibility for the streamlined probate process available in many
states. Chapter 6 will discuss probate in more detail.

A completed estate planning worksheet also benefits your executor. After your death, your executor can use it to help ensure that all of
your assets have been accounted for.

The Asset Inventory Section of the Worksheet

To complete the asset inventory section of the estate worksheet,
list and clearly describe each of the assets you own, either 100 percent

or as a partial owner. List personal property of significant value, such as fine jewelry, furniture and vehicles, as well as real property, which includes raw land, your home and other buildings you own. Also, list any business interest you have as a sole proprietor, partner or principal in a corporation. Figure 2.2 lists more specific examples of what you might include in this section of the worksheet.

FIGURE 2.2

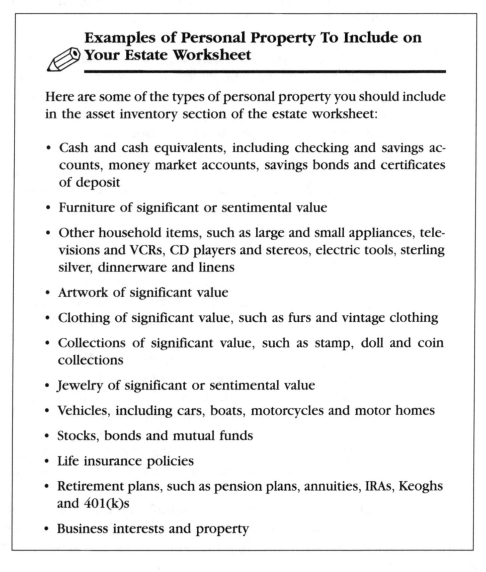

Examples of Personal Property To Include on Your Estate Worksheet

Here are some of the types of personal property you should include in the asset inventory section of the estate worksheet:

- Cash and cash equivalents, including checking and savings accounts, money market accounts, savings bonds and certificates of deposit

- Furniture of significant or sentimental value

- Other household items, such as large and small appliances, televisions and VCRs, CD players and stereos, electric tools, sterling silver, dinnerware and linens

- Artwork of significant value

- Clothing of significant value, such as furs and vintage clothing

- Collections of significant value, such as stamp, doll and coin collections

- Jewelry of significant or sentimental value

- Vehicles, including cars, boats, motorcycles and motor homes

- Stocks, bonds and mutual funds

- Life insurance policies

- Retirement plans, such as pension plans, annuities, IRAs, Keoghs and 401(k)s

- Business interests and property

Describing Your Assets

When you list an asset on the worksheet, describe it using words that clearly indicate what you are referring to. Don't make your executor guess what you're talking about. Some suggestions for describing your personal property follow.

Checking and savings accounts and cash equivalents. Include an account number for each as well as the name and address of the applicable bank or institution.

Furniture. If you have any furniture of value, including antiques, family heirlooms or collectible pieces, provide a short but precise description of each item. If a particular era or style is associated with a furniture item, such as a Chippendale chair or an art deco table, include that information on the inventory worksheet.

Other household items. You may want to group certain types of items together rather than listing each item individually. For example, "All the cooking and kitchen supplies at *(your address)*" or "All the hand tools and electric tools at *(your address)."*

Artwork. Indicate on the worksheet the artist and particular era or style of any significant paintings, sculptures or other artwork you own. Miscellaneous, less important artwork can be identified with a single description, such as "All the paintings and other artwork at *(your address)."*

Clothing. List furs, expensive designer clothes or significant items of vintage clothing separately, and describe them in as much detail as possible, including the name of the designer, if known, any special distinguishing characteristics and the era of the item of clothing, if vintage. Less valuable clothing can be grouped together unless you want to single out any one item. Describe all of the items you group together as "All the items of female (or male) clothing at *(your address)."*

Collections. If you have a significant collection of stamps, coins, books, dolls, antique pens or autographs, for example, describe the collection briefly, including the number of items in the collection and the era of items in the collection, such as "salt and pepper shakers from the 1920s and 1930s" or "antique china dolls from the 19th century."

Jewelry. If you own fine jewelry or family heirlooms, list each item, specifying what it's made of—gold, silver, types of stones—and the era of the item. If you own a collection of good quality, collectible costume jewelry, you may want to list it as a single item—"All the costume jewelry at *(your address)"*—unless some of the items can be considered antiques of value and therefore should be listed separately.

Vehicles. List each vehicle separately, providing a brief description and noting its year of manufacture and license number or other identifying number.

Stocks and mutual funds. For each, include the name of the company, number of shares, relevant CUSIP number, relevant account number and name of the company serving the account.

Bonds. Note the name of the relevant company or government entity, cost of each bond purchased and date purchased.

Life insurance policies. Include the policy number and name of the insurance company for each policy.

Retirement plans. Note the type of plan or benefit, any applicable account number and the company administering the plan or benefit.

Business interests. If you have an interest in a business, specify the type of business, the amount of your ownership (if your business is a sole proprietorship, you own 100 percent) and the name and location of the business. If you have an interest in a corporation, indicate the number of shares you own.

Land and buildings, including your home. List the complete address of each piece of property you own. If you own raw land without a specific address, indicate the number of acres you own and their approximate location, including the town, city or county. If you name a county only, indicate the town or city closest to the acreage.

If you own a second home, such as a lake house, and you intend to leave both the home and its furnishings to a beneficiary, include the home's furnishings in your description of the property—for example, "Vacation home and all furnishings located at *(address of your vacation home).*"

Type of Ownership

Referring back to Chapter 1 as necessary, indicate how you own each of the assets on your worksheet. As a quick review, you may own an asset by yourself 100 percent, as a joint tenant with right of survivorship, as a tenant by the entirety or as a tenant in common. In addition, an asset is either separate or community property. Recording this information will help you pinpoint the assets you can and cannot include in your will.

To save time and space when completing this section of the worksheet, you may want to abbreviate each type of ownership. For example:

Joint tenant with right of survivorship .... J.T.W.R.O.S.
Tenant by the entirety .... T.E.
Tenant in common .... T.C.
Community property .... C.P.
Separate property .... S.P.

Because you have already designated beneficiaries for assets like life insurance policies, employee benefits plans, IRAs and Keoghs, you cannot transfer these assets with a will. Therefore, enter the abbreviation D.B. (designated beneficiary) in the "Type of Ownership" column where appropriate.

Percentage of Your Ownership

In the column titled "Percentage of Your Ownership," indicate what percentage of each asset you own. For example, that figure will be 100 percent if you own the asset yourself and something less if you own the asset with one or more people.

Net Value of Your Ownership

In the final column of the worksheet, record the current market value of each asset you've listed. *Current market value* is what you could sell the asset for today. The value of a bank account is simply the amount of money in the account. You should be able to determine the market value of an employee benefits plan, a Keogh or an IRA by calling the plan administrator or provider.

If you own antiques or artwork that you feel is of significant worth but you're unsure of its exact value, you might want to have it appraised. That way, the asset won't be undervalued or overvalued.

If you own a business or have an interest in one, include the value of your business interest on the worksheet. To determine the value, it's best to consult with an experienced certified public accountant. As an overview, however, if your business is a sole proprietorship, its value is what you could sell the business for. If you're involved in a partnership or a limited liability corporation, the method of compensating deceased or retiring owners and the liquidation value of your interest in the business are both possible determinants of the value of your interest. If you have an interest in a corporation, take into account the value of your shares of the business as well as any buy-out agreements that may be in effect.

 **HOT TIP**

If you're a business owner, issues like the potential impact of your death on the business's ability to continue functioning as a going concern and how you will be compensated at retirement for your interest in the business affect the value of your interest.

Don't worry if some of your asset valuations are approximations. Unless you pull numbers out of thin air, reasonably approximate valuations should not create problems.

The Liability Inventory Section of the Worksheet

Your liabilities can include any outstanding bank or personal loans you're obligated to pay, credit card and bankcard debt, property liens, debts to the IRS, judgments rendered against you and past-due child support or alimony payments. Don't worry about small debts like your monthly utility bills.

Liabilities can also include your share of any outstanding debts related to an asset you may own with others. For example, let's assume you own a beach house with two friends as joint tenants and the market value of the house is $90,000. Let's also assume that the balance on the beach house mortgage is $30,000 and that you and your co-owners also owe $5,000 in back taxes. Therefore, your share of the total debt associated with the beach house would be $11,667 because you have a one-third interest in the property.

When you complete the liability section of your worksheet, be sure to include relevant account numbers as well as the names and addresses of the companies, government agencies or individuals to whom you owe money.

The Estimated Net Value of Your Estate

To determine the estimated net value of your estate, add the values of all the assets you list on your worksheet and subtract from that the total value of the liabilities you list. If the net value is less than $600,000, you need not worry about federal estate taxes, although state estate taxes may be of concern. If the figure is more than $600,000, talk with your attorney about what you can do to minimize your tax liability.

Plan to review and update your estate planning worksheet on a regular basis. During your life, it's likely that you will gain and also lose or sell assets; your assets may appreciate or depreciate in value; and you may take on new debt or pay off existing debt. These changes will affect your net worth and the kind of estate planning you may need to do.

 **HOT TIP**

Everything Your Heirs Need To Know, 2nd edition, by David S. Magee (Dearborn) is a personal recordkeeping organizer that enables you to gather into one simple volume an abundance of important documents and data regarding your assets, family history and final wishes.

FIGURE 2.3

Your Estate Planning Worksheet

ASSET INVENTORY			
Description of Asset	Type of Ownership	Percentage of Your Ownership	Net Value of Your Ownership
1.			
2.			
3.			
4.			
5.			
6.			
7.			

Total Current Value of Assets $

LIABILITY INVENTORY	
Description of Liability	Amount You Owe (Your Share of Liability)
1.	
2.	
3.	
4.	
5.	
6.	
7.	

Total Current Liabilities $

	Total Assets	$
	Less	
	Total Liabilities	$
	Total Value of Estate:	$

CHAPTER THREE

Selecting Your Executor and Beneficiaries

When you write your will, you have three crucial decisions to make:

1. Who to name as executor of your estate
2. Who to leave your property to—your beneficiaries
3. What to give each beneficiary

This chapter will help you make these decisions by explaining the role and duties of an executor, the factors to consider when choosing one and the issues to review when deciding on your beneficiaries.

A blast aboard a Navy ship during World War I almost ended the film career of a person who would be one of Hollywood's most famous and talented actors—Humphrey Bogart. The young son of a doctor, Bogart was badly injured, his face scarred and his upper lip partially paralyzed. The tough guy look that resulted served him well in his career.

Bogart started his film career portraying killers, but he really made his mark playing tough guys with a tender heart. His most famous role was Rick in *Casablanca,* the guy who let his love go off with another man then left to fight in World War II. He starred in *To Have and Have Not* in 1944, the same year he married Lauren Bacall, his wife until his death on January 14, 1957.

In preparing his will, Bogart faced the same dilemma everyone does when writing a will—who to pick as executor. Most people choose just one executor. However, Bogey picked three! In addition to his wife, he designated his friend, A. Morgan Maree, Jr., and Security First National Bank of Los Angeles. (See Figure 3.1.)

What Is an Executor?

An *executor* is the person you choose to act as legal representative of your estate after you die. Your executor works with the probate court to carry out five key tasks for your estate:

1. Locate your will
2. Collect your assets
3. Pay legitimate creditor claims
4. Pay any taxes your estate owes
5. Distribute your assets to your beneficiaries

You must designate your executor in your will. Many people choose their spouse for this duty; however, if he or she is in poor health or is elderly, someone else would probably be a better choice. Instead, you might designate an older child, another family member or a close friend. Keep in mind, if your estate is large or complex, or if

FIGURE 3.1

Humphrey Bogart: Net Estate Table
Prominent Actor, Los Angeles, California

GROSS ESTATE **$910,146**

Debts	*$101,768*
Administrative Expenses	*3,988*
Attorney Fees	*11,249*
Executor Fees	*11,249*
Calif. Inheritance Tax	*21,325*
Fed. Estate Tax*	*124,655*

TOTAL COSTS **$274,234**

NET ESTATE **$635,912**

---

*$380,284 marital deduction

---

problems with your will crop up after you die, an executor's job can be time consuming and stressful. Choose an executor who can bear this potential burden.

Also name a substitute or an *alternate executor* in your will. This person assumes executor duties should your first choice be unable or unwilling to act as your executor after you die. This happened in Humphrey Bogart's case. Lauren Bacall Bogart renounced her right to act as executrix of her husband's estate, so an alternate was needed.

Your executor is legally entitled to receive a fee for acting as your legal representative; the fee will be paid by your estate. However, if you don't want your executor to receive a fee, you can stipulate that in your will.

If your executor is a close friend or one of your beneficiaries, he or she probably will want to waive the fee. On the other hand, if your executor is to receive the same share of your estate as your other beneficiaries, you may want to insist that he or she accept a fee so that you don't feel like you're taking advantage of your executor. Discuss the issue of a fee with the person you want as your executor. For example,

HOT TIP

Be explicit in your will about whether you want your executor to receive a fee. If your will is silent on the subject, most states will provide for one, usually making the fee a percentage of the value of your estate.

Doris Duke specified that Bernard Lafferty, her butler and executor, should receive $5 million for administering her estate!

Some states require that executors be bonded. If this is the case in your state, you may be able to waive that requirement in your will. If you can, more money will remain for your beneficiaries because the cost of the bond would have been deducted from your estate.

 **HOT TIP**

Even if you waive the bonding requirement, your state may require a cash bond if your executor lives out of state.

Professional Executors

Some people prefer to use a professional executor, usually a bank or an attorney. Because professional executors charge a substantial amount of money for their services—money that will be paid by your estate—using a professional does not usually make economic sense for a small to modest estate. However, a professional can be a wise choice if your estate is large and complex and especially if you're concerned that your will may trigger intrafamily squabbles that might make serving as executor an especially stressful experience for a nonprofessional. A professional executor may also be able to save your estate money and hassles during probate. Finally, opt for a professional as your executor if you can trust no one in your life to do a good job in that role. As mentioned earlier, Humphrey Bogart included a professional among his executors—Security First National Bank of Los Angeles.

Coexecutors

Rather than naming one person to act as executor, you may want to appoint coexecutors. Sometimes this is done so that all of the responsibilities of executor don't fall on the shoulders of one person. Also, coexecutors can be a good idea if your first choice for executor doesn't live nearby. The coexecutor who lives closer to home can help with the day-to-day details of administering your estate. Be aware, however, that this arrangement can be impractical because probate-related documents that require both executors to sign will mean sending these papers back and forth, which could slow the probate process.

Some experts suggest that if you choose a professional executor, you name a family member or close friend as coexecutor. The rationale is that having a coexecutor who is attuned to the needs and interests of your family can reassure family members.

What To Look for in an Executor

The job of executor brings with it many important responsibilities. A good one can save your estate money, make the probate process easier for your family and help resolve any problems that may arise during the probate process as quickly and as inexpensively as possible. Therefore, when evaluating possible executors, think in terms of someone who enjoys the trust and respect of your family and who is conscientious, well organized and fair-minded. Also, don't choose someone intimidated by lawyers, paperwork and bureaucracies.

Another important qualification for an executor is a willingness to do the job. Therefore, don't designate someone as your executor until

---

 **HOT TIP**

If you are a business owner, you might want to choose an executor or a coexecutor with experience running your particular kind of business.

you have reviewed the responsibilities of the job with that person and you are absolutely certain that he or she wishes to assume them.

Your executor must be an adult and a U.S. citizen. Also, he or she cannot be a convicted felon.

After you die, your executor must be formally approved by the probate court. Although unlikely, if the court denies approval, it can appoint someone else.

Duties of an Executor

Exactly what must your executor do? The list below runs down some of an executor's more typical duties. These describe what an executor would probably have to do if your estate goes through the traditional, formal probate process rather than the less formal probate process some states now allow for certain types of estates. For a discussion of both types of probate, see Chapter 6.

- Notify all interested parties of your death and the terms of your will.
- Inventory all of your assets and determine their values.
- Pay any claims, including outstanding debts and estate taxes, using the assets in your estate. This may require selling estate assets.
- Manage your investments. This includes liquidating assets as appropriate.
- Help defend your will against any contests.
- Meet the reporting requirements of the probate court.
- Disburse assets to your beneficiaries according to the terms of your will.

 **HOT TIP**

In most states, an executor is personally responsible for all estate tax liabilities to the extent of the estate and for any late filings.

Most executors use an estate attorney to help them through the probate process. However, because an attorney's fees can be substantial and will be paid by your estate, it's a good idea to talk over with your executor when legal help would be appropriate. If you would like your executor to use a particular attorney or law firm, say so; however, you cannot *require* your executor to do so.

Notice the substantial administrative fees incurred by Mahalia Jackson's estate (see Figure 3.2). In covering them, this famous gospel singer's estate was reduced by one-fifth. Possible explanations for the magnitude of those fees include tax problems, legal problems and professional advisers who took advantage of Jackson.

Be aware of the specific powers your state gives to executors, as well as any restrictions your state imposes on them. If need be, you can

FIGURE 3.2

Mahalia Jackson: Net Estate Table
Celebrated Gospel Singer, Chicago, Illinois

GROSS ESTATE	**$563,445**
Debts	*$28,000*
Administrative Expenses	*44,973*
Attorney Fees	*22,500*
Executor Fees	*33,870*
Ill. Inheritance and Estate Tax	*12,896*
Calif. Inheritance Tax	*5,405*
Fed. Estate Tax*	*96,082*
TOTAL COSTS	**$243,726**
CASH IN ESTATE	**$202,000**
NET ESTATE	**$319,719**

*No marital deduction

Charitable bequest of $5,000

 **HOT TIP**

The heirs to your estate can hold your executor personally responsible for diminishing your estate's value if they can prove that it was due to the executor's neglect, breach of duties or deliberate actions.

grant your executor additional powers in your will. Depending on your state, those additional powers might include the right to make real estate transactions on behalf of your estate and the ability to borrow money to pay your estate's debts.

What You Can Do To Make Your Executor's Job Easier

Obviously, your executor will perform an important service for you and your family. Therefore, while you are alive, you should do whatever you can to make that person's future job as easy as possible. This means taking the actions listed in Figure 3.3.

Your Beneficiaries

Your *beneficiaries* are the individuals and organizations you leave your property to. They can include your spouse and children, other family members, close friends, your alma mater, a favorite charity or even a cherished pet! Your beneficiaries may or may not be your *heirs*—the people legally entitled by the laws of your state to inherit from you.

On the surface, deciding on your beneficiaries and what you want to leave each of them may seem like a simple process that you can accomplish quickly. And it often is. However, it's helpful to spend time thinking about what you own, what you would like to accomplish through your gifts and the possible consequences of each gift. That way, you can be certain that you put your gifts to their best use and that

FIGURE 3.3

✓ Details That Will Make Your Executor's Job Easier

❑ Be sure your will is legally valid.

❑ Review your will with your executor, and answer any questions he or she has.

❑ Let your executor know where you keep your will, and give him or her an unsigned copy. If your will is in a home safe or safe-deposit box, tell your executor where you keep the combination or key. If you revise your will or revoke it and write a new one, make sure your executor has a copy of the revisions or the new will.

❑ Explicitly state in your will that you expect your executor to hire professionals as needed to help him or her carry out the duties of executor. Doing so will discourage your beneficiaries from complaining if the executor uses the services of an attorney, a CPA or an appraiser, for example.

❑ Give your executor a copy of your estate planning worksheet.

❑ Explain your rationale for any unusual bequests, for treating your children differently, for disinheriting someone or for anything else in your will that may create confusion or controversy after you die, possibly delaying completion of the probate process.

❑ Maintain complete and well-organized records related to your personal finances, property and investments, and let your executor know where you keep them. These records include your Social Security number, income tax returns, real estate records, insurance policies, bank accounts, debt documentation, credit card account numbers, ownership papers and a list of expected death benefits, to name a few.

FIGURE 3.3 (continued)

✔ Details That Will Make Your Executor's Job Easier

❑ Provide your executor with pertinent information regarding your personal life and family history. That information should include the name of your current spouse, your marriage certificate, the names of any previous spouses as well as your divorce papers, your birth certificate, your naturalization papers, your military records and the names and addresses of any children, grandchildren, adoptive children, stepchildren or children born out of wedlock.

❑ If you own a business or have an interest in one, make sure your executor knows where all pertinent records are and what you want done with your business after you die. If you have a trusted employee with whom you want your executor to work, give your executor that person's name and phone number and let your employee know what you've done.

❑ Give your executor the names, addresses and phone numbers of your attorney, CPA, banker and other personal advisers.

❑ Write out your desires for your burial or cremation as well as any specific arrangements you have made. Be as detailed as possible. Give your executor a copy, along with your spouse or unmarried partner.

❑ If you have made arrangements for any of your organs to be donated after your death, list them in writing and include the name, address and phone number of the organization you donate to. Give a copy to your executor and to your spouse or unmarried partner.

you identify and deal with any possible problems or conflicts a gift might create before you die. Ask yourself the following questions:

- Whom do I want as my beneficiaries?
- Do any of them have special needs?
- Do I want to treat all of my children the same, or do I have good reasons to treat them differently?
- Do I want to leave everything to my spouse? Will that cause him or her tax problems? If so, what can we do now about that potential problem?
- Do I want my beneficiaries to have full control of what I leave them when I die or as soon as they turn age 18 or 21? (If you wish them to wait, you may want to use a trust rather than a will to give away your property.)
- How can I ensure that the children from my first marriage receive some of my property when I die?
- Is my spouse a responsible money manager?
- Are any of the gifts I want to leave to a particular beneficiary likely to spark controversy and discord among my heirs—maybe even a contest to my will?
- Can I make someone's life happier and more secure with a special gift?

Your answers to these and other questions may help you prepare your will and also may suggest that you need to use other estate planning tools besides a will. This is something to discuss with your attorney.

Whenever you designate a beneficiary for a specific asset, it's a good idea to name an *alternate beneficiary,* too, especially if the pri-

 **HOT TIP**

A beneficiary can *disclaim* or turn down an asset you leave him or her. This might happen if the gift will create tax problems for your beneficiary or if one of your creditors has a substantial claim attached to the asset and your beneficiary would have to pay the debt if he or she accepted the gift.

mary beneficiary is elderly or ill. That way, if the primary beneficiary dies, there will be no question about who should receive the property instead.

Rather than naming specific beneficiaries, you may want to leave certain property to a class of beneficiaries and then define exactly whom you include in that class. This is especially appropriate if you name your children as beneficiaries of your will. For example, you might want to leave certain assets to "All of my children," then define exactly whom that includes.

Be sure to designate a *residual beneficiary* and alternate in your will. The residual beneficiary receives all assets in your estate not left to a specific beneficiary. This allows for the possibility that you may overlook an asset or fail to amend your will to include a new asset. Otherwise, your state will determine who receives any asset not specifically left to someone in your will.

 **HOT TIP**

Rather than naming an alternate beneficiary for each asset, you can stipulate in your will that property should go to your residual beneficiary should the primary beneficiary die.

For example Humphrey Bogart, a smooth talker all his life, died of throat cancer. In his will, he created the Humphrey Bogart Foundation to fund grants "for medical research with special attention to the field of cancer." The remainder of his estate went to this organization.

 **HOT TIP**

It is not uncommon to direct in a will that all estate-related taxes, fees and debts be paid out of the residuary estate and that whatever is left over be given to the residual beneficiary.

Naming Your Spouse as a Beneficiary

If you are married and living in a community property state, you and your spouse each has an undivided interest in one-half of all your community property. This was explained in Chapter 1. Each spouse's one-half interest is unaffected by the death of the other. To ensure that your spouse gets your share, you must specifically name him or her as beneficiary of that property in your will. Otherwise, your spouse may end up legally owning with another relative, your child perhaps, a share of important assets like your home or automobile. This could create problems for your spouse if he or she doesn't get along with the new co-owner or disagrees with the co-owner about what to do with it. For example, your spouse might be prevented from selling the asset or borrowing against it if the other owner refuses to cooperate.

📝 HOT TIP

If your spouse cosigned on a note, and the note is outstanding at the time of your death, and your estate does not have enough funds to pay it, the creditor can try to collect from your spouse. In community property states, your spouse may be liable even if he or she wasn't a cosignator.

If you live in a separate property state, the law says that when you die, your surviving spouse is entitled to a fixed amount of your estate. If you don't leave your spouse at least that amount, separate property states would allow your spouse to "take against your will." That means that your spouse can take the portion of your estate that represents your state's minimum. Interestingly, in his will, Humphrey Bogart advised his wife not to take against the will because he thought her interests would be better served if she accepted the terms of his will.

Naming Your Minor Children as Beneficiaries

All states limit the amount of property that a minor child can legally own without adult supervision. Usually, this amount is in the range of $2,500 to $5,000. Therefore, if you want to leave your young child more than your state's maximum in your will, you must designate a property guardian for that child. The property guardian will manage your child's property until he or she reaches the age of 18 or 21, depending on your state. Turn to Chapter 5 to learn more about leaving money and other property to children.

Naming Charitable Organizations as Beneficiaries

You may use your will to leave money or property to a charitable organization for a general or specific purpose. If the organization is an IRS-approved charity, your gift is exempt from federal gift and estate taxes and from the same taxes in most states.

When writing your will, be sure that you list the charitable organization's complete legal name and its exact address. Otherwise, you may unintentionally benefit the wrong organization. You may also want to contact the charity you plan to benefit to find out whether it has a *planned giving program.* This program can tell you about your giving options, information that you can then review with your attorney.

The District of Columbia, Florida, Georgia, Idaho, Mississippi, Montana and Ohio all impose restrictions on charitable gift giving through wills. Although they vary from state to state, possible restrictions include limits on the total dollar amount someone can leave to a charity in his or her will—often no more than a certain percentage of the total value of the estate—and requirements that a charitable gift not be made within a certain period of time prior to the willmaker's death. If you live in a state that imposes restrictions on charitable gift giving and you want to remember a charity in your will, talk to a qualified estate planner or estate attorney.

Remembering Your Pet

You can even remember Fido in your will, with restrictions. In most states, you cannot leave property directly to a pet nor can you set up a trust for a pet in the animal's name. However, you can leave money in your will to a family member or friend and stipulate that it be used to care for your pet after your death. Another much more expensive option is to establish a trust in the friend's or family member's name and specify in the trust document what the funds are to be used for.

✎ HOT TIP
_____

Be sure that your friend or family member is willing to care for your pet.

Special Messages and Explanations

You can include special messages in your will. For example, you might want to say how much you love someone or tell each family member what you most appreciate about him or her. If you're like most people, you may not have many valuable assets to give to the important people in your life, so the messages in your will can serve as your gifts—final expressions of your feelings for them. For some people, such messages mean more than any tangible asset you may leave them.

It is usually not a good idea to explain in your will why you are not leaving a specific gift to someone, especially if the explanation involves anything negative or potentially embarrassing for the person. Remember, a will is a public document that anyone can read. To include something negative or embarrassing about someone in your will exposes your estate to the possibility of being sued for libel. A better approach is to tell the person while you are still alive that you're not giving certain property to him or her and explain why. Provide your executor with an explanation, too.

Explanations can be a good idea if you are concerned that your will may trigger discord among your heirs and beneficiaries or even will contests. For example, you might tell your children that you don't plan to leave equal shares of your estate to each. If your will includes nothing for one of your heirs or you leave a significant amount of property to someone who is not an heir, you also need to explain. Finally, discuss unusual gifts to individuals or organizations.

Again, however, make these explanations to the affected individuals and to your executor before you die, and be careful that what you say in your will does not put your estate at risk for a libel suit.

Giving Options

As you think about your beneficiaries and the property you own, don't forget that certain types of assets automatically convey to beneficiaries outside your will and that you have other ways of transferring assets to beneficiaries aside from using your will. If you need to review the types of assets that can and cannot be transferred to others with a will, return to Chapter 1. Chapter 4 will review estate planning tools other than wills. See Figure 3.4 for a net estate table on philanthropist Nelson A. Rockefeller.

FIGURE 3.4

Nelson A. Rockefeller: Net Estate Table
Philanthropist, Former New York Governor,
Former U.S. Vice President, New York, New York

GROSS ESTATE	**$79,249,475**
Debts	*$12,835,883*
Administrative Expenses	*5,616,896*
N.Y. Estate Tax	*640,291*
*Fed. Estate Tax**	*3,428,777*
TOTAL COSTS	**$22,521,847**
NET ESTATE	**$56,727,628**

*Federal estate tax includes a $23,600,372 marital deduction and a $35,302,036 deduction for charitable bequests.

If You Want To Do More Than Write a Will

As Chapter 1 explained, depending on your estate planning needs and concerns, you may want to use more than a will to accomplish your estate planning goals. Therefore, this chapter will introduce some other estate planning tools you should know about, explain when and why a particular tool might be appropriate and provide an overview of each tool's advantages and disadvantages.

An Overview of Estate Planning Tools

Understanding the range of estate planning tools available to you and under what circumstances they might be appropriate will not only help you make informed decisions when working with your attorney; the knowledge can also help protect you from unscrupulous individuals who try to sell you estate planning you don't need.

At the time this book was written, various parties were contesting the will of one of the wealthiest women in the world. Doris Duke, a tobacco heiress, left behind a very complicated will and estate as well as many questions about her condition at the time she wrote her will, the intentions of the people in her life during her last years and the circumstances of her death. We can expect to see legal battles related to Duke's estate for some time to come.

If her will is any indication, Duke was an interesting and unusual person. For example, Duke gave her eyes to the Eye Bank for Sight Restoration; asked to be buried at sea; and created a trust of $100,000 for the "care, feeding, comfort, maintenance and medical treatment" of her dog.

Another interesting aspect of her will was that Duke listed people who owed her money and specifically forgave their debts, all but one. The one debt she didn't forgive was the $5 million she loaned to Imelda Marcos, wife of the former president of the Philippines.

The estate planning tools that will be discussed in this chapter are

- joint ownership of assets;
- *inter vivos* gifts;
- life insurance;
- employee benefits and other retirement plans;
- payable-on-death and trust accounts; and
- trusts, both testamentary and living.

An overview of their primary advantages and disadvantages compared to wills appears in Figure 4.1. Each of the tools listed in this figure will be discussed in a subsequent section of this chapter. Chapter 9 addresses two additional tools, living wills and durable powers of attorney.

Joint Tenancy

Owning assets with someone else as joint tenants with right of survivorship is an inexpensive and simple estate planning tool. As explained

FIGURE 4.1

Comparing the Advantages and Disadvantages of Key Estate Planning Tools

Tool	Advantages	Disadvantages
Will	• Easy to prepare and relatively inexpensive • Allows you to name a personal and a property guardian for a minor child • Can be modified at any time up to your death	• Property in a will is subject to probate • A minor who is a beneficiary automatically receives the property you've left him or her when the minor turns age 18 or 21 • Probate can be time consuming and expensive in some states
Joint tenancy	• Inexpensive and simple to use • Avoids probate	• You don't fully control an asset you own as a joint tenant • May be gift taxes involved in making a solely owned asset a joint asset
Inter vivos gift	• Helps reduce the size of an estate for probate and tax purposes	• You lose use of the property you give away
Life insurance	• Safe, secure way to build an estate • Avoids probate • No income tax liability associated with benefits • Good way to provide liquidity for estate	• No flexibility in how or when death benefits are paid to policy beneficiary
Employee benefits	• Death benefits avoid probate	• No flexibility in how benefits are paid to beneficiary • Have tax consequences

FIGURE 4.1 (continued)

Comparing the Advantages and Disadvantages of Key Estate Planning Tools

Tool	Advantages	Disadvantages
POD account and trust account	• Usually are revocable • Inexpensive and easy to set up • Account funds avoid probate	• No flexibility in how or when account funds are paid to beneficiary
Testamentary trust	• Provides tax advantages • You can control when trust beneficiary receives trust assets • Not established until you die	• Trust assets go through probate before reaching trust
Revocable living trust	• Avoids probate • You have control of trust assets while you are alive • You can control when trust beneficiary receives income trust income and assets • You can be both trustee and beneficiary of trust	• Relatively expensive to set up • No tax advantages
Irrevocable living trust	• Avoids probate • Tax advantages • You can control when trust beneficiary receives income from trust	• Relatively expensive to set up • Once an asset is placed in an irrevocable trust, it can't be removed or changed in any other way

in Chapter 1, if you and another person own property as joint tenants, when you die, your share automatically passes to your co-owner. Therefore, assets owned as joint tenants with right of survivorship need not be included in your will and do not go through probate.

Spouses frequently own property like a home or a bank account as joint tenants. However, you can also own property as a joint tenant with another relative, your unmarried partner or a close friend, for example.

The first provision in Humphrey Bogart's will indicates that the home he shared with his wife, Lauren Bacall Bogart, was owned by them as joint tenants. All other property he considered to be community property.

Another type of joint ownership very similar to joint tenancy is tenancy by the entirety. The major difference between the two is that the latter applies only to property owned by spouses. Real estate and bank accounts are commonly owned this way.

Before you rush off to make all of your assets joint assets, with a beneficiary as your co-owner, be aware that potential drawbacks to this form of ownership include the following:

- *When you share ownership of an asset, you don't have full control over it.* For example, if you want to sell the asset and your co-owner balks, you won't be able to execute the sale. Also, your co-owner can give away his or her share or even lose it in a legal judgment. (Your co-owner's creditors could come after his or her share of an asset you own together as payment of a debt the co-owner owes, for instance.) If either were to happen, it's possible that you could find yourself owning an asset with someone you don't know! Even worse, if the joint asset is real estate, your co-owner could force you to sell your share of the property. Obviously, if you choose to be a joint owner with someone, you should trust and get along with one another.
- *If you decide that you no longer want to own an asset as a joint tenant, it can be extremely difficult—if not impossible— to change the nature of the ownership.*
- *If you change an asset you own by yourself into a joint asset by giving a share of it to someone, you may be subject to a federal gift tax.* This does not apply if you give the share to your spouse.

- *Some states freeze funds in joint bank accounts after one of the joint account holders dies.* To regain access to the account, the other account owner must present certain legal documents. If the other account owner is your surviving spouse and if he or she needs the account funds to pay bills, take care of household expenses or help pay for your funeral and burial, the delay could be a hardship.
- *Assets like jewelry that do not have legal documents evidencing ownership can be difficult to convert into jointly owned assets.*
- *Joint ownership can negatively affect the eligibility of a spouse for Medicaid.* This can be a serious problem if a spouse needs long-term care and does not have private long-term care insurance. If long-term care may be of concern to you or your spouse in the near future, consult with an attorney familiar with elder law or check with someone else familiar with Medicaid rules before making an asset a joint asset or ending a joint ownership arrangement. Also, consider purchasing long-term care insurance.
- *Joint ownership can create tax problems for husbands and wives with substantial estates.*

Giving Away Your Property While You Are Still Alive

Many people give money and other property to their beneficiaries while the gift givers are still alive. That way, they have the pleasure of giving and of knowing how much the recipients benefit from and appreciate the gifts. Other people have more practical reasons for making gifts while they're alive. For example, a person may want to minimize the assets in his or her estate that must go through probate so the process can be completed more quickly or so the estate can qualify for the quicker and cheaper probate process many states make available as an alternative to the formal probate process. Others want to minimize the size of their taxable estates.

The federal government says that you may give up to $10,000 each year to as many individuals or charities as you want without paying a gift tax. If married people make gifts together, the limit is $20,000 annually. So if you have two children, every year you and your spouse together can give both of them as much as $40,000 without having to pay taxes. *Inter vivos* gifts can also be made to trusts.

For a gift to provide tax benefits, it must be an irrevocable gift; that is, you cannot take it back. Also, it must be a completed gift. This means that once you make the gift, you no longer retain any ownership rights to it or control it in any way and the new owner has full possession of it. A future interest in something provides you with no tax benefits.

To make sure that a gift will provide tax benefits, be sure to document it properly. For example, if you give away real property such as real estate or a car, you must change the name of the owner on all ownership papers, give those papers to the new owner and file all required paperwork with the courts in the new owner's name. If the gift is an intangible, such as stocks and bonds or bank accounts, provide the new owner with the certificates or account passbooks, for example, and make sure that his or her name is on all related documents.

HOT TIP

Putting the title to a piece of property in someone else's name and then keeping the new title rather than giving it to the person whose name is now on the title does not qualify you for tax benefits from that gift. It is not viewed as a completed gift because the title is still in your possession.

When you write your will, you may want to specify that the value of any gifts your beneficiaries have already received from you should not be viewed by the court as an advance on what you've left them in your will. If you don't stipulate this, your beneficiaries may not receive all that you intend. The same advice applies to trusts and *inter vivos* gifts.

Life Insurance

Life insurance policies are very safe ways to build an estate over time, to provide for a beneficiary and to give your estate liquidity. After you die, that liquidity can be used to help pay probate-related costs, debts and taxes.

As long as the beneficiary of your policy is not your estate, when you die, the policy proceeds will not go through probate, which means they will be immediately available. If your estate is the beneficiary, the proceeds will not be subject only to probate but to creditor claims as well.

A life insurance policy offers two more potential advantages. First, if it's payable to your spouse or to a dependent, in most states the proceeds will be protected from any claims creditors have against your estate. Second, policy proceeds may be exempt from your state's inheritance taxes.

FIGURE 4.2

Arthur W. Bush: Net Estate Table
A Founder of the Nunn-Bush Co., Shoe Manufacturer, Milwaukee, Wisconsin

GROSS ESTATE*	**$579,648**

Debts	*$5,225*
Administrative Expenses	*17,112*
Attorney Fees	*15,400*
Executor Fees	*9,505*
Wis. Inheritance Tax	*29,378*
Fed. Estate Tax**	*56,411*

TOTAL COSTS	**$133,031**
CASH IN ESTATE	**$19,477**
NET ESTATE	**$446,617**

*Included in the gross estate is $48,985 of **business life insurance** payable to Nunn-Bush Co. and $75,779 of **life insurance** deemed the property of the widow.

**$251,514 marital deduction

The main disadvantage of an insurance policy as an estate planning tool is its inflexibility. As a policyholder, you cannot specify when, after your death, the insurance company should begin payments to your beneficiary, nor can you define the amount of each payment. All of those things are set by the policy itself.

Lack of flexibility could be a problem if the value of your death benefits is substantial and if your beneficiary is not a good money manager. In the worst-case scenario, your beneficiary may quickly squander each payment, leaving him or her without enough income to pay for expenses until the next payment arrives.

 **HOT TIP**

You can get around a policy's lack of flexibility by placing your policy in a trust.

Instead of buying policies that pay a series of death benefits over time, people with substantial estates often purchase life insurance policies that pay a single lump-sum death benefit. The single payment is used to pay estate taxes, fees and other estate-related expenses.

Employee Benefits

Employee benefits and individual retirement accounts (IRAs) are common estate planning tools. Employee benefits include pension plans, annuities, profit-sharing plans, stock bonus and employee stock ownership plans, 401(k)s and Keogh plans.

Typically, employee benefits plans and IRAs pay you a retirement income while you're alive—your lifetime benefits—and also provide an income—your death benefits—to your designated beneficiary after you die. Read the documentation related to your employee benefits or IRA or talk with the plan administrator to find out how and when your benefits are paid.

Having the death benefits of your employee benefits plan or IRA paid to a beneficiary over time in a series of regular payments, like an annuity, can be a good way to help that person pay his or her living and other expenses. Generally, the death benefits provided by both types of estate planning tools do not go through probate. The exception is if you name your estate as beneficiary.

Like that of life insurance plans, the primary disadvantage of employee benefits plans and IRAs as estate planning tools is their lack of flexibility in regard to how and when your beneficiary receives his or her benefits. However, as with insurance, setting up a trust to receive the benefits can eliminate this disadvantage.

Payable-on-Death Accounts and Trust Accounts

Payable-on-death (POD) accounts and trust accounts are inexpensive, easy-to-use estate planning tools. Neither is affected by probate, and both are practical alternatives to a trust for people with modest estates.

A *POD account* is established simply by opening one at a bank or another authorized financial institution, such as a brokerage house. When you do, you must designate a beneficiary for the account. As long as you are alive, you are the account owner. If you and your spouse or another person, like your oldest child, open the account together, you'll be co-owners and the account will function much like a joint bank account. POD accounts are recognized by most states, but some states place limits on them.

Like a POD account, a *trust account* is set up and maintained at a bank or another authorized financial institution and has a designated beneficiary (or beneficiaries). Your estate can be a beneficiary, too.

Trust accounts can also have more than one owner or trustee. Plus, in the document establishing the trust account, you can specify another person who may make account transactions on your behalf, even if you become mentally or physically incapacitated.

A trust account is usually revocable unless the account document clearly states otherwise. If it's irrevocable, once you put funds in it, you can't take them out because they no longer belong to you; they belong to the account trustee.

The primary disadvantage of POD and trust accounts is their lack of flexibility. When you die, the assets in either of these accounts will be paid in full to their beneficiary unless the beneficiary is a minor. Therefore, these estate planning tools are usually not appropriate for giving away substantial amounts of money, stocks and bonds, for example.

 **HOT TIP**

In some states, the probate court can take the funds in POD and trust accounts to pay estate-related taxes, fees and debts if the money in your estate does not cover them.

Trusts

A *trust* is a legal entity into which you place property you want to go to a beneficiary. Two basic kinds of trusts exist: testamentary trusts and living trusts, sometimes called *inter vivos* trusts.

A *testamentary trust* is part of your will. Prior to your death, it exists only on paper, but after you die, the trust becomes activated and the assets you've earmarked for it go through probate, are transferred into the trust and are then distributed to the trust's beneficiary. A testamentary trust is always irrevocable, which means that once you die, the trust cannot be revoked or changed in any way.

Testamentary trusts are inexpensive and easy to establish; in fact, it's a good idea for anyone with minor children to include a testamentary trust in his or her will to help provide for the children if both parents die. Testamentary trusts also provide tax advantages. However, the assets in a testamentary trust go through probate. An example of a testamentary trust is the trust Doris Duke set up for her dog.

 **HOT TIP**

If you want a living trust to be revocable, make its revocability explicit in the trust document.

Living trusts are not part of your will and are created while you live. They can be revocable or irrevocable, but most are revocable.

Trusts are not unlike corporations in that they have a legal existence separate from the person who creates them. You need the help of an attorney to set up a trust because it is a complicated legal entity and should always be coordinated with the rest of your estate plan.

 **HOT TIP**

Before establishing any type of trust, weigh its benefits against its costs and compare both to those of other estate planning tools you may be considering.

A trust can be set up to do just about anything as long as it doesn't conflict with the laws of your state and it doesn't promote anything that would be considered poor public policy. See Figure 4.3 for examples of some of the more common types of trusts.

More than any other estate planning tool, a trust gives you control over whatever you give to a beneficiary, even after you die. That's one of the reasons trusts are so useful and popular. You can create a trust for a very specific purpose, and you can stipulate exactly when and under what conditions its beneficiary receives the assets in it. You can use almost any criteria you want, including the financial needs, age, maturity, physical or mental limitations and money management abilities of the trust's beneficiary.

Doris Duke's will is a good example of the many ways trusts can be used. She created the Doris Duke Foundation for the Preservation of Endangered Species of All Kinds, Both Flora and Fauna, from Becoming Extinct and gave her two camels, two horses and donkey to the foundation. Duke also created the Doris Duke Charitable Foundation. This trust had several purposes, including contributing to the assistance of actors, dancers, singers, musicians and other artists of the entertainment world in fulfilling their ambitions and providing opportunities for the public presentation of their arts and talents; preserving wildlife; promoting medical research to cure major diseases; and helping any

FIGURE 4.3

✏️ Examples of Common Types of Trusts

Two basic types of trusts exist: testamentary trusts and living trusts. Within these two categories are many specific kinds of trusts—some with a very general purpose and others with a very narrow purpose. To give you a feel for the variety of trusts, here are some of the more common:

- *Insurance trusts* are created to purchase life insurance and to provide tax benefits.

- *Spendthrift trusts* are established to manage funds for a beneficiary you feel does not have the ability to manage the money and other property you give him or her. For example, the person could be a poor money manager, developmentally challenged or mentally ill.

- *By-pass trusts* allow you to pass a total of $600,000 to anyone you want while you are alive or at your death without being subject to taxes.

- *Qualified terminable interest property (QTIP) trusts* can help you provide for children by a previous spouse and for your current spouse. This trust allows your current spouse to benefit from trust income while he or she is alive. After your spouse dies, the trust property goes to your children from your previous marriage. It can also be used for other purposes.

- *Charitable trusts* can be set up to make regular gifts to a charity. This kind of trust provides tax benefits.

- *Standby trusts* are set up while you live but are not funded until after you die. They may be funded by the proceeds from your life insurance policy or retirement benefits, for example. The assets in standby trusts avoid probate.

- *Grantor-retained annuity trusts* are irrevocable trusts commonly used to transfer ownership of a closely held business. It allows the current owner to retain business income and control and also reduces federal income taxes.

- *Medicaid-qualifying trusts* can help make you eligible for nursing home care under the federal Medicaid program without having to substantially reduce the value of your estate. This means you are able to retain much of your estate to pass on to your beneficiaries.

organization actively promoting antivivisectionism. Perhaps Duke's most unusual trust was the one she established to benefit her dog.

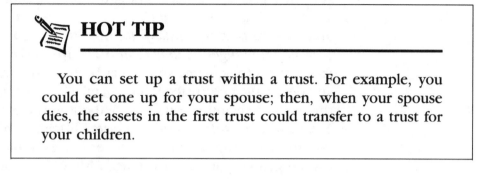

HOT TIP

You can set up a trust within a trust. For example, you could set one up for your spouse; then, when your spouse dies, the assets in the first trust could transfer to a trust for your children.

To illustrate just how flexible a trust can be, here are some situations when a trust could be useful:

- *Both you and your spouse die while your child is still a minor.* You want to ensure that the property your child inherits is managed in a way that maximizes its value and provides financially for your child until your child can take charge of his or her own finances. If you place the property in a trust, the trustee you name to manage the property will not have to contend with the restrictions and requirements that the state places on a property guardian.

- *You leave your teenage children a substantial amount of money.* If you die, you don't want them to gain full control of the money when they turn 18 years old, as they would if you left them the funds in your will, because you don't think they'll be mature enough to manage it responsibly at that age. However, if you create a trust for them, you can stipulate when they take control of the money and the amount of trust income they receive each year up to that point. In Elvis Presley's will, he created a trust for his daughter, Lisa Marie Presley. When Lisa Marie turned 25 years old, the trust ended and she got all of the assets in the trust.

- *Your child is mentally handicapped and unable to earn an income or manage money.* You can establish a trust to ensure that he or she is financially well cared for without jeopardizing any government benefits your child receives.

- *Your spouse is younger than you and likely to outlive you.* However, he or she is a poor money manager. A trust helps make sure that your spouse will not squander the money and other assets you leave him or her.
- *Your health is failing and you know that at some point soon you may no longer be able to manage your own finances.* You can set up a trust, name yourself as both trustee and beneficiary and designate a cotrustee who will take over for you, managing things in the manner you've spelled out in the trust document.
- *You own real estate in multiple states.* Placing it in a trust allows you to avoid probate in each state. For example, Doris Duke owned property in various states. Although she was a resident of New Jersey, she requested that her estate be probated in New York State.
- *You want to leave your children a vacation home and want to be sure that no conflict will arise over its use.* You also want to be sure that if it is sold, the proceeds are divided fairly among your children. You can specify all of this in a trust agreement.
- *You plan on leaving all of your property to your spouse, but you are concerned that he or she may not pass on a share of that property to your children from a previous marriage.* A trust helps you address this concern.
- *You want to reduce your estate taxes or minimize the amount of your estate that goes through probate.* Again, a trust is the answer.

To create a trust, you must prepare a trust agreement. This document states the purpose of the trust and should spell out key details regarding the trust, including those listed in Figure 4.4.

 **HOT TIP**

Some trusts now include incentive clauses. For example, if the trust beneficiary earns a certain amount of money during a specified period of time, he or she receives a certain amount of property from the trust.

FIGURE 4.4

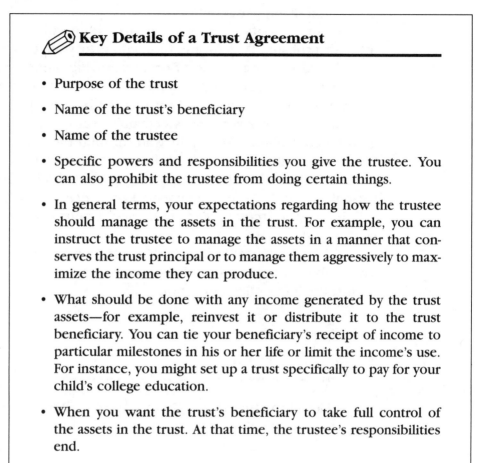

✏️ **Key Details of a Trust Agreement**

- Purpose of the trust

- Name of the trust's beneficiary

- Name of the trustee

- Specific powers and responsibilities you give the trustee. You can also prohibit the trustee from doing certain things.

- In general terms, your expectations regarding how the trustee should manage the assets in the trust. For example, you can instruct the trustee to manage the assets in a manner that conserves the trust principal or to manage them aggressively to maximize the income they can produce.

- What should be done with any income generated by the trust assets—for example, reinvest it or distribute it to the trust beneficiary. You can tie your beneficiary's receipt of income to particular milestones in his or her life or limit the income's use. For instance, you might set up a trust specifically to pay for your child's college education.

- When you want the trust's beneficiary to take full control of the assets in the trust. At that time, the trustee's responsibilities end.

More about Living Trusts

Assets commonly placed in a living trust include wholly owned stocks, bonds, life insurance and real estate. Although retirement accounts, such as IRAs, Keoghs, pension plans and 401(k)s, cannot be placed in a living trust, a living trust can be their beneficiary. However, such an arrangement makes the living trust liable for income taxes. Although an individual who is the beneficiary of such assets also is liable for income taxes, he or she can get an extended payout of that tax debt; a living trust cannot.

Because a living trust is not part of your will, its assets don't go through probate. That means they come to your beneficiaries more quickly and reduce the cost of probate, saving money for your estate. An exception to this rule exists, however. If you don't place any assets in a revocable living trust before you die because you want it to be funded after your death, the assets you've earmarked for the trust will go through probate. You might want to fund the trust in this manner because you don't or can't afford to incur the time and expense required to fund the living trust while you are still alive. To fund a living trust after you die, you must create a *pour over will* within your will. Talk to your attorney to learn more about pour over wills, which are usually unnecessary.

Although revocable living trusts offer estates no tax advantages, irrevocable trusts do. They also provide estates with some protection against creditor collection actions.

HOT TIP

Despite all the advantages of a living trust, it does not eliminate your need for a will. (See Figure 4.5 for more on this.)

The Trustee

The person you designate as trustee will manage the trust property on behalf of its beneficiary according to the instructions you set out in the trust agreement.

The person you choose as trustee should exhibit good financial sense and sound judgment. Depending on the kind of trust you create and the value and complexity of the assets you place in it, these traits can be even more critical for the trustee than for your executor. For example, if you establish a trust to provide for your spouse after you die, your trustee may have responsibility for managing the trust prop-

FIGURE 4.5

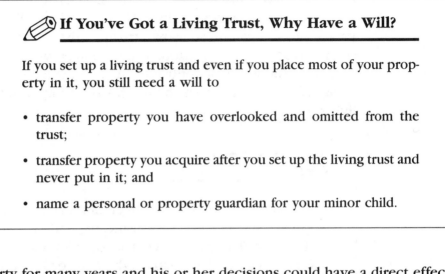

If You've Got a Living Trust, Why Have a Will?

If you set up a living trust and even if you place most of your property in it, you still need a will to

- transfer property you have overlooked and omitted from the trust;

- transfer property you acquire after you set up the living trust and never put in it; and

- name a personal or property guardian for your minor child.

erty for many years and his or her decisions could have a direct effect on the long-term financial well-being of your spouse.

Obviously, the trustee should be someone you have great confidence in. This person could be a family member, a close friend, a bank trust department or a trust company.

HOT TIP

If the trustee's responsibilities will continue for years, you might designate a professional trustee because working with a bank or trust company can help ensure trust asset management of consistent quality.

Be sure to name an alternate or a successor trustee in case your first choice for trustee is not able to carry out his or her duties.

Trustees are eligible to receive a fee for their services. It will be either a flat fee or a percentage of the value of the trust's assets, depending on your state. Many nonprofessional trustees waive this fee, but professional trustees do not.

When you set up a living trust, you must transfer legal ownership of any asset you place in it to the trustee. That means you no longer own the asset; the trustee does. However, depending on the laws of your state, you can be your own trustee. Also, in most states, you can be the trust's beneficiary, too. The advantage of wearing both hats is that you maintain total control of the trust assets while you are alive, using and benefiting from them. This is an important advantage of a living trust.

 **HOT TIP**

If you name yourself as trustee of a living trust, be sure to appoint a successor or a cotrustee, depending on the purpose of the trust. This person will take over if for some reason you are no longer able to manage the trust or if you die.

Transferring ownership of assets to the trustee can be a time-consuming and potentially expensive process. Also, the banks and title companies involved may want to review the trust agreement to confirm that the trustee has been given the power necessary to manage all assets in the trust. Although many people use attorneys to help them with the ownership transfer process, you can reduce the costs of a living trust by handling the transfers yourself.

An attorney will charge you at least $1,000 to set up a living trust. This price does not include the costs involved in legally transferring property to the trustee and any associated fees. To decide whether a living trust is an appropriate estate planning tool for you, consult with a qualified attorney. Your decision should be based on, among other things, an analysis of your estate planning goals, the assets you own, the needs of your beneficiaries and a comparison of the cost of a living trust to that of other estate planning tools you could use. For example, if you consider using a revocable living trust to avoid probate, be sure to compare the costs of setting up the trust to the costs your estate would incur if the assets you place in the trust go through probate. These days, because most states have created a less expensive and faster probate process as an alternative to the formal probate process, most people find that probate avoidance alone is not a cost-effective reason for setting up a living trust.

Taxes and Living Trusts

If you set up a revocable living trust and name yourself as trustee, you'll be considered the owner of the trust property for federal income, estate and gift tax purposes. This means you must report all income produced by the trust assets on your annual tax return, and you may have to pay taxes on that income.

While you're alive, any transfers from the trust to its beneficiary will be treated as *inter vivos* gifts from you. If you exceed your annual per-person *inter vivos* gift maximum, your estate will be taxed on the amount exceeding it.

When you die, all of the property in the revocable living trust will be considered part of your gross taxable estate. (See Figure 4.6 for more advantages and disadvantages of a revocable living trust.)

On the other hand, an irrevocable living trust is treated as a separate tax entity for income, estate and gift tax purposes. A separate tax return must be filed each year for the trust. Income from the trust's assets generally is taxable to the trust, not to you. For federal gift tax purposes, transfers of trust income or principal to someone else will not be treated as gifts from you. When you die, the trust property will not be included in your taxable estate.

Living Trusts Are Not Panaceas

It's time for a note of caution about living trusts. In recent years, they have become extremely popular and are often touted as *the answer* to estate planning for everyday Americans. However, as this book has already made clear, they are not the best option for everyone. Most people can find better and cheaper ways to achieve certain estate planning goals.

Furthermore, incidences of living trust fraud are common. (See Figure 4.7.) Often, the victims didn't need living trusts but were convinced by unscrupulous salespeople that trusts rather than wills were the best estate planning tools for them. Sometimes these victims die without either a valid trust or a valid will, not realizing that a trust does

FIGURE 4.6

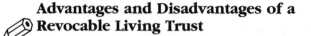

Advantages and Disadvantages of a Revocable Living Trust

Before setting up a revocable living trust, be aware of its pros and cons.

Advantages

- It gives you maximum flexibility and control in regard to when and under what conditions your beneficiary receives the trust assets.

- Trust assets don't go through probate.

- You can be both trustee and beneficiary, controlling and benefiting from the assets in the trust.

- It's harder for any disgruntled heirs to challenge a living trust than a will.

Disadvantages

- It's still necessary to have a will.

- Your family will not receive a family allowance while it waits to receive assets from the trust.

- A living trust is a relatively expensive estate planning tool compared to other tools.

- The trust provides no protection from your creditors.

- It offers no income or estate tax advantages.

not obviate the need for a will. As discussed earlier, even if you have a valid trust, a will serves as a backup for any property that you did not include in the trust or that you acquire after you set up the trust. Also, you cannot use a trust to designate a personal or property guardian for your minor children. You can do that only with a will.

FIGURE 4.7

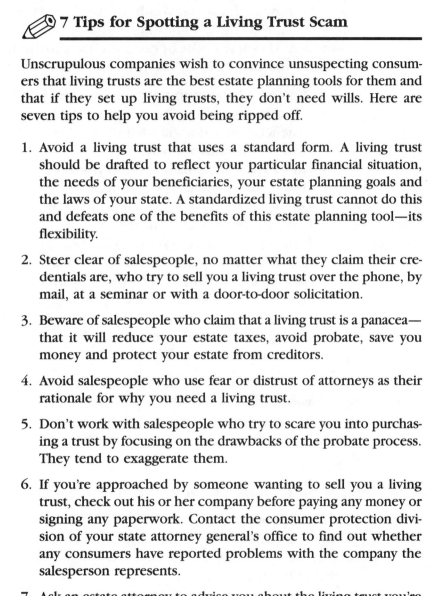

7 Tips for Spotting a Living Trust Scam

Unscrupulous companies wish to convince unsuspecting consumers that living trusts are the best estate planning tools for them and that if they set up living trusts, they don't need wills. Here are seven tips to help you avoid being ripped off.

1. Avoid a living trust that uses a standard form. A living trust should be drafted to reflect your particular financial situation, the needs of your beneficiaries, your estate planning goals and the laws of your state. A standardized living trust cannot do this and defeats one of the benefits of this estate planning tool—its flexibility.

2. Steer clear of salespeople, no matter what they claim their credentials are, who try to sell you a living trust over the phone, by mail, at a seminar or with a door-to-door solicitation.

3. Beware of salespeople who claim that a living trust is a panacea—that it will reduce your estate taxes, avoid probate, save you money and protect your estate from creditors.

4. Avoid salespeople who use fear or distrust of attorneys as their rationale for why you need a living trust.

5. Don't work with salespeople who try to scare you into purchasing a trust by focusing on the drawbacks of the probate process. They tend to exaggerate them.

6. If you're approached by someone wanting to sell you a living trust, check out his or her company before paying any money or signing any paperwork. Contact the consumer protection division of your state attorney general's office to find out whether any consumers have reported problems with the company the salesperson represents.

7. Ask an estate attorney to advise you about the living trust you're considering before you commit to it.

Estate Planning if You're a Business Owner

If you own a business, you have special estate planning issues to address. Some of those issues depend on the legal structure of your business, as do some of the options you have for addressing them. The questions you may have to ask yourself include the following:

- What will happen to my business after I die?
- If I want my business to continue as a source of income for my beneficiaries, who will own it and who will manage it?
- How will I transfer ownership?
- Do I have a succession plan in place?
- How will my business be valued?
- Do I want my business to go through probate? If not, what can I do to protect it from probate?
- How will my estate taxes be paid? (For many people, their business is their most valuable asset. Lack of adequate tax planning may force your family to sell your business or liquidate important assets to pay estate taxes unless you have made other provisions.)
- If I want my business sold or liquidated rather than continued as a going concern, what can I do now to prepare for those transactions?

The help of an estate attorney with specific experience dealing with businesses is critical. To prepare you for working with your attorney, the rest of this chapter will review some of the issues to consider and will provide an overview of some of your options.

How the Legal Form of Your Business Affects Estate Planning

If your business is a sole proprietorship, you may be its only employee. Therefore, when a sole proprietor dies, the business often dies, too, because its viability is based totally on its owner's skills, knowledge and business contacts.

When estate planning, you—as a sole proprietor—have several options regarding the future of your business. First, you can find someone else to take it over. Or you can sell the business. This might be possible if your business has substantial assets and if your client list is valuable. Finally, you might arrange for liquidation of your business's assets after you die. This is a viable alternative only if you have substantial assets.

If you own your business with others as a partnership or a corporation, what happens to your share of the business after you die and how much your share is worth are things you can't decide alone because other owners are in the picture. Instead, they should be spelled out in business agreements like partnership agreements, buy-sell agreements, shareholders' agreements and so on. These kinds of agreements can establish an up-front value for your share of the business and can create an automatic market for it.

If You Want Your Business To Continue Operating

If your business is a sole proprietorship or a family business, and if you want it to continue after you die, you must identify your successor. That person could come from within your family, from the ranks of your employees or from outside your business.

To ensure a smooth transition from you to your successor, it's best to have a written plan. This plan should address the future management and ownership of the business, the roles and responsibilities of the future owner and other relevant financial and legal business issues. When developing this plan, ask yourself the following questions:

- Who will have primary decision-making responsibility for the business?
- How should business profits be apportioned?
- Should those family members most actively involved in running the business realize a greater share of the profits than those owners less actively involved?
- If the business is incorporated, should some family members have voting stock and others have nonvoting stock?
- If the business is sold after I die, should my beneficiaries have continued roles in the business? If so, what should these roles be?
- How should such a sale be structured?

If your business will continue after you die, and if you rely on it to provide either short-term or long-term income to your family, it's a good idea to identify your successor while you're alive. This way, you can provide that person with the training and on-the-job experience necessary to fill your shoes and you can be assured that your successor has the skills and personal qualities necessary to run your business.

HOT TIP

You may want to give your successor the legal power to run your business in the event you become mentally or physically incapacitated and are no longer able to make business decisions for yourself.

If your successor is one of your children, and if your business is a closely held corporation and you own all the shares, one decision you must make is whether to leave either the entire business or a majority interest to that child. If you leave the whole business to that child, in the interest of fairness, you should give your other children property of equal value or structure some other financial arrangement to provide for them. You'll face the same fairness issue if one of your children takes over your sole proprietorship or your share of a partnership.

HOT TIP

Key person insurance is a good way to provide funds for the continued operation of a business after the owner's death and until a successor is in place.

When planning the future of your business, it's always best to openly discuss the subject with your family. Make sure everyone feels comfortable with your plans so that after you die, intrafamily discord won't surface, possibly jeopardizing the stability of your business.

Transferring Ownership

If your family-owned partnership or corporation will continue operating after your death, and if you want to give your children or spouse your share of the business, you must decide how best to transfer ownership. For example, if your business is incorporated, you can give family members shares of stock, possibly as annual *inter vivos* gifts. This option has the advantage of helping to reduce the size of your estate for tax purposes.

You can also leave your business or your share of a business to your spouse and take advantage of the unlimited marital tax deduction. However, as Chapter 6 points out, although this approach provides your estate with tax benefits, it can create future estate tax problems for your spouse. This also applies to sole proprietorships.

Another option is to leave the family member who will own your business enough stock to buy out the rest of your estate. This is often accomplished by buying a life insurance policy and naming that person the policy beneficiary. This also applies to sole proprietorships.

Liquidation

If you have no successor, if you don't want your business to continue after your death or if it is unlikely that it could continue as a viable business after your death given the critical role you play in it, liquidation of its assets may be the best option after you die.

To prepare for liquidation, develop and update regularly an inventory of your business assets, including your accounts receivables. The inventory should include a value for each asset. It is also a good idea to include with the inventory a list of reputable business liquidators, including their names, addresses and phone numbers, so your family will not have to do this research themselves after your death. Keep the inventory with your will.

Estate Taxes

As already indicated in this chapter, it's not uncommon for a business or a share of a business to be the most significant asset in a person's estate and for that asset to create a substantial estate tax liability. Sadly, many business owners fail to adequately plan how their estate taxes will be paid. As a result, to pay those taxes, a family is sometimes forced to sell the very asset the business owner anticipated would provide a good living for the spouse or children after the business owner's death. Therefore, it's important to meet with a qualified CPA or tax attorney to discuss how your business fits into your estate planning and what you can do to minimize estate taxes and protect your business. Following are just a few possible tax minimization strategies:

- *If your business is a corporation, you could give away up to $10,000 worth of stock each year to each of your children or to others ($20,000 a year if you and your spouse both make the gifts).* This would help reduce the value of your estate.
- *You can leave your business to your surviving spouse, taking advantage of the unlimited marital deduction.* However, if you do this, you'll be passing the buck to your spouse because your spouse will have nothing to protect his or her estate from taxes, depending on the estate's value at the time your spouse dies. One way to avoid this problem is to place all or part of your business in a by-pass trust, with your spouse as beneficiary.
- *You can sell your company to your children or to whomever you wish while you're alive.* However, you must pay taxes on the profit you realize from the sale.
- *You can establish a grantor-retained annuity trust (GRAT) if your business is closely held.* This irrevocable trust not only will provide your estate with federal tax benefits but also will pay you a fixed amount of money for a specified period of time. When that time is up, the assets in the trust—company stock or other income-producing assets—will transfer to the trust beneficiary.

Edward S. Harkness was left a fortune built from oil, and he spent his life giving it away. Harkness made recorded charitable and educational gifts of $117,741,101 and unrecorded gifts of more than $100 million. Because of these bequests, his estate taxes were reduced. (See Figure 4.8.)

Probate and Your Business

When planning your estate, you may want to take steps to protect it from the probate process, depending on how your business is structured. For example, if it's a sole proprietorship or if you own all the

FIGURE 4.8

Edward S. Harkness: Net Estate Table
Railway Financier, Heir to Vast Oil Fortune and
Philanthropist, New York, New York

GROSS ESTATE **$97,070,933**

Debts	*$2,273,425*
Fees and Administrative Expenses	*1,282,619*
Conn. Inheritance Tax	*9,090*
Ohio Inheritance Tax	*4,161*
N.Y. Estate Tax	*10,773,225*
Fed. Estate Tax*	*26,627,875*

TOTAL COSTS **$40,970,395**

CASH IN ESTATE **$2,062,996**

NET ESTATE **$56,100,538**

---

*$41,364,207 marital deduction

---

stock, during the probate process, the court may inhibit efficient business decision making and your business could be damaged as a result. A good way to avoid probate is to place your business in a living trust; another option is to own it as a joint tenant.

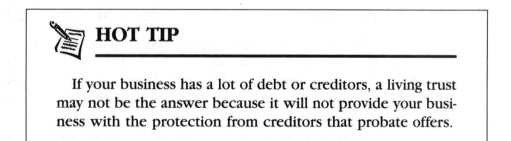

HOT TIP

If your business has a lot of debt or creditors, a living trust may not be the answer because it will not provide your business with the protection from creditors that probate offers.

CHAPTER
FIVE

Your Children and Your Estate

Parents of minor children face special issues and concerns when planning their estates. This chapter will explain those issues and concerns and will review options for addressing them. It will also discuss issues related to leaving property to adult children.

Naming a Personal Guardian for Your Minor Child

This book has already explained that if you're the parent of a minor child, in some states, the only way you can legally designate someone to raise that child should both you and your spouse die is through your will. The person you name in your will is called a *personal guardian.*

You should designate a substitute personal guardian, too. This person would take over in the event your first choice for guardian is unable or unwilling to carry out the responsibility.

On Valentine's Day 1994, Jerry Garcia, leader of the Grateful Dead rock band, married his third wife, Carolyn Koons. On May 12, 1994, he signed his last will. A little more than a year later, on August 9th, Garcia died.

Garcia was legendary at his death. His music and the man himself attracted a myriad of followers over a 30-year career, including "Deadheads," the name given to his most ardent fans. When he died, his fans and many others mourned his loss. To many of us, he was a link to the counterculture revolution of the 1960s.

Although we associate Garcia with the counterculture, he wrote a very traditional will that showed great concern for his family. For example, he appointed Sunshine May Walker Kesey as guardian of his minor child, Keelin Garcia. She would be the person to raise Keelin if her mother, Manasha Matheson, did not survive him.

HOT TIP

Some states allow parents to designate a personal guardian for their minor child outside of their will.

You can name two people as coguardians for your young child. This arrangement can make sense if the coguardians are married. However, in a society where an estimated 50 percent of all marriages fail, you may be creating the potential for problems down the road if the

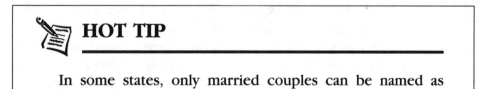

HOT TIP

In some states, only married couples can be named as coguardians.

couple you appoint splits up. Thus, if you want to name coguardians, contact a lawyer first.

If you have more than one young child, you can name a different guardian for each child. Whether this makes sense for you depends on your family's particular situation.

As Chapter 1 indicated, if your minor child does not have a legal guardian, but a family member or close friend acts as *de facto* guardian, that status may not create problems until the unofficial guardian tries to add the child to the family health insurance policy, enroll the child in school or arrange surgery for the child that requires the consent of the minor's parent or legal guardian. These are just a few examples of instances when not appointing a legal guardian for a young child could create problems. In such situations, the *de facto* guardian must initiate a legal process to become official guardian and to gain all of the powers he or she needs to raise your child.

If the court is asked to appoint a personal guardian for a minor child, unless it has good reason to do otherwise, the court will usually name the unofficial guardian or another family member willing to raise the child. This means that the adult who raises your child may not be someone you would have chosen had you designated a guardian yourself.

 **HOT TIP**

In some states, you can stipulate whom you do *not* want to serve as your child's guardian in addition to whom you do want.

After you die, the court in your area must confirm the appointment of your child's guardian. Generally, unless someone comes forward to contest the appointment, the confirmation process goes smoothly. Should problems develop, however, a hearing will be held and the court will base its choice of the right guardian on what it feels would be in the best interest of your child.

 **HOT TIP**

If you expect that a guardianship may be contested, it's a good idea to leave money in your will to help the estate pay for an attorney's help.

If You Are Divorced or Separated

If you are divorced or separated and have custody of your child when you die, by law, your minor child's other parent ordinarily assumes full responsibility for the child. However, should this parent also die, in most cases, the person your spouse names as your child's personal guardian would raise the child.

If you would prefer that your ex-spouse not raise your child, you can say so in your will and name the person you prefer. However, because your reasons for making this request are probably not flattering to your ex, it's usually not a good idea to state them in your will. If you do, your ex-spouse may sue your estate for libel. Instead, you may want to provide your executor with a written statement of your reasons and other pertinent documentation. It is also a good idea, if you have the resources, to leave money in your will for your executor or a beneficiary to pursue a contest of guardianship should your ex-spouse begin raising your child despite your wishes.

Even if you state your preference in your will, the judge probably will award custody of your child to your ex-spouse unless that person doesn't want the responsibility or it can be demonstrated that your ex-spouse would be an unfit parent due to a history of serious problems with drugs or alcohol, a criminal record or a history of mental illness, for example. An argument could also be made that your ex-spouse would be an unfit parent if he or she had not seen or taken an interest in your child for an extended period of time.

If you want to do what you can to ensure that your ex-spouse does not gain custody of your minor child, talk with an attorney who specializes in family law. Remember, though, it's a long shot.

Qualities To Look For When Choosing a Personal Guardian

It goes without saying that the person you choose as your young child's personal guardian should be someone of good character whom you trust to do a responsible and caring job of raising your child. The person should also be someone who shares your basic values and who will respect any special concerns you have about how your child is brought up. For example, you may want your child to be raised in a specific religion. Obviously, when choosing a guardian, you want to avoid someone with a drug or an alcohol problem or with a history of emotional problems. Most important, the person you choose should have the time and willingness to take on the responsibilities of the job. Therefore, before naming a guardian, make sure that he or she is willing to take on the job.

It is almost never a good idea to name a minor child's grandparent as guardian. Grandparents are more likely than younger adults to become seriously ill and to die while the child is still a minor. From a very practical day-to-day perspective, grandparents often do not have the energy necessary to raise a young, active child. Also, the generation gap can make it difficult for grandparents to cope successfully with any issues and problems their minor charge faces.

If your child is old enough to have opinions on the subject, talk with him or her about guardians you are considering. Listen carefully if your child raises serious objections to a potential guardian.

Leaving Property to a Minor Child

Jerry Garcia was quite specific in his will about what his children would receive from his estate after he died. For example, he gave his youngest child, Keelin Garcia, half-interest in a house he owned, along with a share of his estate.

On the other hand, Clark Gable, a famous movie star best remembered as Rhett Butler in the movie *Gone with the Wind,* never included his child in his will.

While Gable was filming his final movie *The Misfits* with Marilyn Monroe, his wife announced she was pregnant. In the will in effect at the time, Gable had declared that he had no children, although stories contradicted this statement. Five months later, Gable died suddenly.

By all accounts, Gable was looking forward to the birth of his child, telling everyone he hoped it would be a son. In fact, he said that when his son was born, he planned to retire and spend the rest of his life taking care of the child. Unfortunately, Gable died before he ever saw his son, John Clark Gable, now an actor, and before he had a chance to amend his will to provide for his child. (Gable's will appears in Appendix A. See also Figure 5.1.)

All states limit the maximum amount of property a minor child can legally own without the appointment of an adult to manage and distribute the property for the child. The maximum varies by state but is in the range of $2,500 to $5,000. Therefore, if you leave your minor child property valued at more than your state's maximum, you must designate an adult to manage the property on your child's behalf.

FIGURE 5.1

Clark Gable: Net Estate Table
Screen Star, Hollywood, California

GROSS ESTATE	**$2,806,526**

Debts	*$328,227*
Administrative Expenses	*319,235*
Attorney Fees	*58,652*
Executor Fees	*Waived*
Calif. Inheritance Tax	*96,365*
Fed. Estate Tax*	*298,559*

TOTAL COSTS	**$1,101,038**
CASH IN ESTATE	**$1,705,488**
NET ESTATE	**$1,705,488**

*$409,180 marital deduction

The reason for the limit is that children younger than 18 or 21, depending on your state, are assumed not to have the knowledge and maturity necessary to manage significant amounts of money or other assets. Also, from a practical perspective, minors are legally prevented from entering into contracts and from buying or selling real estate, stocks, bonds and other property—limitations that hinder their ability to benefit from any significant assets they inherit.

The adult you designate to manage and distribute your child's property will be a property guardian, an account custodian or a trustee, depending on the estate planning tool you use to transfer the property to your child.

You can use five basic estate planning tools to leave property to a minor child:

1. Leave money and other property to your spouse or another adult with the express understanding that it will be used for your child's benefit.
2. Use your will to give money and other property to your minor child, as Jerry Garcia did.
3. Name your child as beneficiary of your insurance policy, employee benefits plan or IRA.
4. Leave money and other property to your minor child through the Uniform Gifts to Minors Acts (UGMA) or the Uniform Transfers to Minors Act (UTMA).
5. Set up a trust for your child.

You may want to use one of these estate planning tools or a combination of these tools. Each will be discussed in a subsequent section of this chapter. Their advantages and disadvantages appear in Figure 5.2.

Leaving Money and Other Property to Another Adult for Your Minor Child's Benefit

An extremely simple option for leaving property to a minor child is to leave it to your spouse or another adult in your will, stipulating that the property must be used for your child's benefit. You can even mandate the specific things the assets may be used for—to help fund your child's college education, for example.

FIGURE 5.2

Advantages and Disadvantages of Options for Transferring Property to a Minor Child

The pros and cons of your primary options for leaving assets to a minor child are summarized below.

Option	Advantages	Disadvantages
1. Leave money and other property in your will to your spouse or another for the benefit of your child	• No need for a property guardian • Involves no extra expense or paperwork	• No guarantee that your child will actually benefit from the money and other property • Assumes that spouse or other is a good financial manager
2. Leave money and other property to your minor child in your will	• Involves no extra expense or paperwork	• Goes through probate • Depending on value of what you leave your child, you must appoint a property guardian • Your child will receive money and other property at age 18 or 21, depending on your state
3. Name your child as beneficiary of your life insurance policy, employee benefits plan, IRA	• Avoids probate • Involves no extra expense or paperwork	• Depending on value of death benefits, you must appoint a property guardian • Your child will have full control of benefits at age 18 or 21, depending on your state

FIGURE 5.2 (continued)

Advantages and Disadvantages of Options for
Transferring Property to a Minor Child

Option	Advantages	Disadvantages
4. Use the UGMA or UTMA	• Custodial accounts are easy to use and relatively inexpensive to set up • Custodian, not property guardian, manages assets	• Irrevocable • In most states, your child will take control of money and other assets at age 18 or 21, depending on your state • You must set up a separate account for each child
5. Set up a trust for your child	• Offers maximum flexibility and control over disbursement of trust income and when child takes control of trust assets • Trustee manages assets in trust	• Relatively expensive to set up • Depending on type of trust, can be time consuming to set up

This option has two advantages. If the value of the assets you've earmarked for your child is more than your child can own legally without an adult being present to manage the assets, you won't have to appoint a property guardian because the assets are going to your spouse or to another adult, not to your minor child. Also, leaving assets to an adult for your child's benefit involves no additional expense or paperwork on your part and imposes no recordkeeping or reporting obligations on the adult to whom you leave the property.

Despite these advantages, this option is not recommended, especially if the value of property you've earmarked for your minor child is substantial. The option gives you absolutely no control over how your child's property will be managed or even whether it will be used to benefit your child, although you can indicate in your will what you hope will be done with the property. The option also assumes that the adult you leave the property to will never use those assets if times get tough and will never borrow against them. It also assumes that if you leave the assets to your spouse and your spouse remarries, he or she will not be pressured by the new spouse to use your minor child's money or property for other purposes. Finally, if the adult you leave the assets to dies without a will, your child has no guarantee of receiving the property.

Leaving Money and Other Property to Your Minor Child

Including your child in your will offers some of the same advantages as the previous option—specifically, it involves no extra paperwork or expense. However, this option comes with some potentially significant drawbacks. First, if the value of the property you leave your minor child exceeds the maximum your state says a young child can legally own without adult supervision, you must designate a property guardian to manage the property. Some states require that property guardians put up a bond, and all states require that they adopt a very conservative investment strategy when managing a minor child's property. For example, Texas limits property guardians to government-backed investments. This strategy may mean that the property guardian cannot maximize the value of your minor child's property. On the other hand, the strategy helps protect your child's assets from high-risk investments. Property guardians will be discussed in greater detail in the next section.

The second drawback of this option is that your child will take full control of the property you leave him or her in your will when the child becomes a legal adult—that is, age 18 or 21, depending on your state. At this age, your child may not be mature or financially savvy enough to manage the assets responsibly, especially if the value of the property you leave to your child is substantial.

Property Guardians

Many times, a married person names his or her spouse as property guardian and designates their child's personal guardian as the alternate. Usually, this arrangement makes sense because the person with responsibility for raising your child should have the resources necessary to do the job. However, before you name your child's personal guardian as the alternate property guardian, make sure that person is a good financial manager and is willing to take on the potential responsibility. After all, the person you choose to raise and nurture your child in the event of your death will not necessarily be good at managing money and other assets or at dealing with the reporting and paperwork all states impose on property guardians.

 **HOT TIP**

Even if you don't use your will to transfer property to a minor child, it's still a good idea to designate a property guardian for your child in the event he or she inherits property from someone else and needs an adult to manage it.

The property guardian must be bonded and is responsible for preparing and filing periodic reports with the court. To comply with these requirements, the property guardian may need the help of an attorney or a CPA. The cost of such professional assistance will be paid from the property you leave your child.

Naming Your Child as Beneficiary of Your Life Insurance Policy, Employee Benefits Plan or IRA

Another way to provide financially for your child in the event of your death is to make him or her the beneficiary of your insurance policy, employee benefits or IRA. At your death, the proceeds from these assets, or death benefits, automatically pass directly to your child, avoiding probate and the claims of creditors.

Depending on the value of the benefits, you must appoint an adult to manage them until your child is a legal adult. Otherwise, they will not be released by the company managing them. The adult will be a trustee, an account custodian or a property guardian, depending on whether you arrange to have the benefits paid directly to your child, placed in a testamentary or living trust or deposited in a custodial account under the Uniform Gifts to Minors Act or the Uniform Transfers to Minors Act, depending on which act your state has adopted.

Using the UGMA or UTMA

The Uniform Gifts to Minors Act (UGMA) was enacted in 1956 but applied only to *inter vivos* gifts of money and securities to minor children. In 1966, the act was amended to include insurance policies and annuities. In 1983, the Uniform Transfers to Minors Act (UTMA) was adopted. This act covers real and tangible property as well as all of the property covered by the 1956 and 1966 versions of the UGMA. Every state has adopted a version of the UGMA or the UTMA.

Using either the UGMA or the UTMA to leave assets to a minor child is simple and inexpensive. All you have to do is open a custodial account at a bank or brokerage house in the name of the person you designate as account custodian and then transfer into the account any assets you want to give your child.

 **HOT TIP**

Be sure that the property you place in a custodial account is not property you might need later. The account is irrevocable.

In addition to their low cost and ease of setup, custodial accounts can have other advantages. First, account custodians do not have to deal with the state oversight and control that property guardians must contend with. Therefore, they can do more to maximize the value of custodial account assets and increase the income they produce.

Second, depending on your state, you may be able to delay beyond 18 or 21, the age at which your child will receive custodial account assets.

However, UGMA and UTMA accounts have some potential disadvantages. For example, when your child becomes a legal adult, he or she will gain full control of property in the account. Depending on the value of the account assets and the maturity of your child at age 18 or 21, this may or may not be a drawback. As noted previously, however, you might be able to extend the custodianship until your child turns 25 years old.

If you have several minor children and you want to use the UGMA or UTMA to leave property to each of them, you must set up a separate custodial account for each child. This is really a very minor disadvantage.

Another drawback is that your minor child must report to the IRS any income or gain earned by the assets in his or her custodial account. That's because your child is their legal owner. If the child is younger than age 14, he or she will be taxed at the *kiddie tax rate*—that is, at your tax rate. When your child reaches age 14, the tax rate will decrease.

Finally, property placed in a custodial account is viewed as a gift. Therefore, if the total of the property transferred to the account in a given year exceeds your annual $10,000 per-person gift limit, you must file a federal gift tax return and the excess will eat into your $600,000 federal tax exemption.

Account Custodians

You may serve as custodian of an UGMA or UTMA account, or you can appoint someone else, such as your child's other parent or a friend. Don't forget to designate a successor custodian, too.

 **HOT TIP**

Although you can appoint a financial institution or a securities broker as account custodian, given the total value of the assets typically placed in a custodial account, doing so is usually not cost effective given the fees a professional will charge.

Account custodians are entitled to receive a fee for their services. However, a relative or close friend may waive the fee.

Account custodians are subject to less state scrutiny and control than are property guardians. They are free to manage account assets and disburse income from an account as needed with little if any court interference.

Setting Up a Trust for Your Minor Child

As you already know, a trust can be an excellent estate planning tool if you leave your minor child a substantial amount of property. Trusts can also be used to convey property to adult children.

The primary benefits of a trust are its flexibility and the amount of control it gives you over the terms of your gift. As Chapter 4 discussed, trusts can be created to respond to almost any estate planning need or concern and, more than any other estate planning tool, they give you the ability to define when your child will receive trust income and when he or she will take full control of trust assets. Such control can be a particular advantage if the value or complexity of the assets you leave your child is considerable.

Another important reason for establishing a trust for a minor child is the independence and power that a trustee has to manage trust assets and dispense income. Trustees don't have to deal with the limitations and reporting requirements faced by property guardians and therefore are freer to maximize the value of trust assets.

Frequently, one parent names the other as trustee. With this arrangement, a minor child's property guardian is often a logical choice for alternate trustee because both jobs require someone who is comfortable dealing with money and investments. Another option is to name the property guardian as primary trustee and someone else as alternate.

To summarize, you can use five basic estate planning tools to leave assets to a minor child. Before you choose a strategy, however, you have to think through many issues. (See Figure 5.3.)

Leaving Property to Adopted Children

When it comes to inheritance, your adopted children, no matter what their ages, have the same rights as your biological children in

FIGURE 5.3

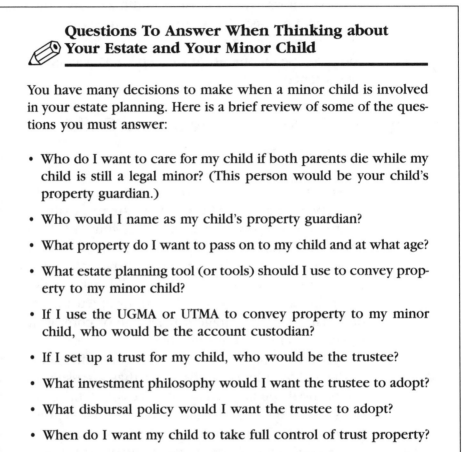

Questions To Answer When Thinking about Your Estate and Your Minor Child

You have many decisions to make when a minor child is involved in your estate planning. Here is a brief review of some of the questions you must answer:

- Who do I want to care for my child if both parents die while my child is still a legal minor? (This person would be your child's property guardian.)

- Who would I name as my child's property guardian?

- What property do I want to pass on to my child and at what age?

- What estate planning tool (or tools) should I use to convey property to my minor child?

- If I use the UGMA or UTMA to convey property to my minor child, who would be the account custodian?

- If I set up a trust for my child, who would be the trustee?

- What investment philosophy would I want the trustee to adopt?

- What disbursal policy would I want the trustee to adopt?

- When do I want my child to take full control of trust property?

- Do I want my minor child to receive income from the trust? If so, for what purposes and how much?

most states. However, if you want to be absolutely certain that your adopted children are treated as well as your biological children, you have two options when writing your will. You can explicitly name each child you leave property to or you can indicate that you leave property to "all of my children" and define what that phrase means, being sure to include your adopted children in the definition.

Yul Brynner, famous for his role in *The King and I,* adopted two Vietnamese orphans, Mia and Melody. Besides making bequests to his biological children, he provided for his adopted children by setting up a trust for them. A legal battle ensued over Brynner's estate after he died. However, attorneys for his adopted children ultimately won for them a settlement from the estate of almost $500,000. (See Figure 5.4.)

If You Have Children from a Prior Marriage

It is common for a spouse to leave all of his or her estate to the surviving spouse. However, if you use your will to do so and you have children from a previous marriage, you have no guarantee that your spouse will pass on those assets to your children, especially if your spouse also has children from a former marriage. This can be of particular concern if your current spouse and your children do not get along.

FIGURE 5.4

Yul Brynner: Net Estate Table
Famed Actor of Stage and Screen, New York, New York

GROSS ESTATE* **$5,000,000**

Debts	*Unknown*
Attorney Fees	*67,000*
Executor Fees	*67,000*
*Fed. Estate Tax [$2,317,100]**	*None*

TOTAL COSTS **$134,000**

NET ESTATE **$4,866,000**

---

*Included in the gross estate is $408,000 of life insurance.

**Full marital deduction (Estimated estate tax without marital deduction)

Figures approximate. Estate not closed at time of this book's publication.

You have a number of ways to deal with this dilemma, and you should certainly raise the issue with your attorney. Possible solutions include the following:

- *You and your spouse can coordinate the provisions of your wills to provide for one another and for any children either of you has from a previous marriage.* However, because a will can be changed at any time, your spouse could amend his or hers after you die, leaving nothing to your children.
- *You can purchase a policy on your life, name your children as policy beneficiaries and set up an irrevocable life insurance trust.* To make this option work, your beneficiaries, not you, should own the policy—that is, it should be in their names, not yours—and you should give them the money every year to pay the insurance premiums. Be careful not to exceed the $10,000 per-person annual maximum for a tax-free gift! Assuming you live at least three years after setting up the trust, when you die, it will not be included in your taxable estate.
- *You can set up a living trust called a qualified terminable interest property (QTIP) trust.* Optimally, this trust would provide income and principal for your spouse and would transfer the trust assets to your children when your spouse dies. Another potential advantage of this kind of trust is that you can use the unlimited marital tax deduction with it; however, a drawback is that your children won't be able to benefit from the assets in the trust until your spouse dies.
- *You can establish separate trusts for your spouse and for your children.* However, given the additional expense involved, this option makes sense only if your estate is substantial and then only if something like a QTIP trust is not practical.
- *You can negotiate a prenuptial or postnuptial agreement with your spouse whereby you both agree in the legally binding contract exactly how your estate will be divided at your death.*

Stepchildren and Your Will

If you have stepchildren, the laws of intestacy do not view them as your legal heirs and they do not have the legal right to inherit from you. Therefore, if you want to make sure they will receive some of your property when you die, make them explicit beneficiaries of your estate planning.

Leaving Property to Out-of-Wedlock Children

In most states, if you're a female and your will leaves property to "all of my children," the laws of intestacy include in that definition any children you have had outside of marriage. On the other hand, if you're a male, the definition will usually include only the children born to you and your wife and those who have proved paternity. However, regardless of your sex and your state, you are free to explicitly include or exclude your out-of-wedlock children in your will. If you have any out-of-wedlock children, it is advisable to consult with an attorney about the intestacy laws of your state.

In his will, Yul Brynner left $25,000 to his daughter, Lark—his child from a love affair he had with a singer in 1958.

Children Born after a Will Is Written

If you use the general phrase "to all of my children" when leaving property to your children in your will, children born after you write it usually inherit the same share of your estate as your other children. Also, nearly all states have laws regarding *pretermitted* children, or children left out of a will. These laws say that a child not included in his or her parent's will is legally entitled to an intestate share of the parent's estate unless it is clear that the omission was intentional. However, the laws vary in regard to the circumstances under which they apply and in regard to how much a pretermitted child can inherit. For example, some laws apply only to children born or adopted after your will is executed, while others apply to all children regardless of when they were born. Check with your estate attorney about the law in your state.

Disinheriting a Child

Let's hope you never have to consider disinheriting a child—that is, leaving a child nothing at all in your will. However, you can do so for just about any reason. Before you disinherit a child, it is a good idea to talk with an estate attorney so that you understand your state's law regarding pretermitted children and you do not run afoul of it.

Typically, the process for disinheriting a child is quite simple: Indicate in your will the exact name of the child you disinherit and explicitly state that the reason your child is not included is that you disinherit him or her. Be sure to talk over your plans with the executor of your estate. You may also want to talk with the child you disinherit.

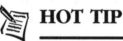 **HOT TIP**

Beware of explaining in your will exactly why you disinherit your child. If you say negative things, you may open your estate to the possibility of a libel suit. A better tact is to give your executor a written statement.

The fact that you don't mention a child in your will may not disinherit that child, it may simply open the door for a will contest after you die. The child you thought you were disinheriting could argue that he or she was just overlooked. If that were to happen, depending on the law in your state regarding pretermitted children, the state would probably award your child some portion of your estate. The exact amount will depend on a number of factors, including whether your spouse is still living and how many other children you have.

 **HOT TIP**

An attorney will probably charge you extra to draw up a will that disinherits your child. That's because your attorney will want to take additional steps to ensure that your desire holds up in court.

One of the most famous examples of someone disinheriting her children can be found in the will of film star Joan Crawford. In her will, Crawford said, "It is my intention to make no provision herein for my son Christopher or my daughter Christina for reasons that are well-known to them." Of course, everyone found out the reasons later when Christina published her best-selling book *Mommie Dearest.*

Christina and Christopher contested Crawford's will. After a legal battle, they reached an agreement with Crawford's estate. Christina and Christopher ended up sharing $55,000 tax free, and Christina got a plaster bust of Joan that was inscribed "To Christina."

Doris Duke also disinherited a child, and her estate was sued as a result. At age 75, Duke adopted 35-year-old Chandi Heffner. They shared common interests in dance, Eastern philosophy and animals. Later, however, their relationship fell apart and was filled with acrimony. Therefore, in her last will, Duke specifically excluded Heffner from receiving anything from her estate, writing, "After giving the matter prolonged and serious consideration, I am convinced that I should not have adopted Chandi Heffner. I have come to the realization that her primary motive was financial gain."

After Duke died, Heffner sued Duke's estate and ended up with a $65 million settlement. As part of the settlement, she agreed not to write a book about her relationship with Duke.

Leaving Property to Adult Children

You can transfer property to your adult children using any of the estate planning tools you might use to give property to any other adult beneficiary. However, depending on your family situation, your estate planning may have to address some special issues related to your adult children. For example, if some of your children are much better off financially than others, or if some have children and others don't, you may not want to leave each of your children the same amount.

Also, if one of your adult children is not a good money manager and you will leave him or her a substantial amount, you may be concerned about how best to ensure that your child doesn't squander the property. A solution is to set up a spendthrift trust, with a trustee in charge of managing and disbursing the trust assets for the adult child. This kind of trust is commonly set up to last until a person turns 50 years old. The thinking is that by this age, even a spendthrift will have matured!

If you have an adult child who is mentally or physically handi-capped and unable to earn a living or manage his or her own finances, you may want to set up a trust to provide for that child throughout his or her life.

CHAPTER SIX

Probate, Taxes and Your Estate

An important goal for many people when they plan their estates is ensuring that the maximum amount of their property goes to their beneficiaries as quickly as possible after they die. Accomplishing this goal can involve minimizing the assets in your estate that go through probate or structuring your estate so that it qualifies for a quicker and cheaper alternative to the traditional probate process; reducing the possibility for creditor claims against your estate; planning for a possible contest; and reducing your estate taxes.

Because the costs and delays of probate can be of concern to estates of all sizes, this chapter will focus most of its attention on the probate process. It will also discuss alternatives to the traditional, formal probate process available to small and modest estates in many states. Finally, the chapter will provide a very general overview of estate taxes and how they can be minimized.

When I was writing this book, a news story appeared about Supreme Court Chief Justice Warren Burger's will. An Arlington, Virginia attorney criticized the extremely simple one-page will as being an example of poor estate planning. Among other things, the attorney claimed that the estate of the Chief Justice would be liable to pay significant estate taxes. Subsequently, however, new information indicated that, in fact, Burger had not done such a bad job of estate planning after all. Although it was not evident from his will, the Chief Justice had set up a living trust and made *inter vivos* gifts as part of his estate planning. These estate planning tools would help save on estate taxes and help decrease the assets that would go through probate.

What Is Probate?

The narrowest definition of *probate* is the legal process of proving the validity of your will after you die so that your property can be distributed to your beneficiaries. However, a broader definition encompasses all of the activities over which the probate court has jurisdiction once you die. This includes determining the validity of your will, formally appointing your executor, gathering together all of the assets in your estate, paying your estate's debts and taxes as well as probate-related fees, and distributing the property in your estate to your beneficiaries.

Assuming that the executor named in your will is approved by the probate court in your county of residence, that person will be responsible for shepherding your estate through the probate process. If the state doesn't approve your choice for executor, it will appoint an administrator for your estate. The court may deny approval if it doesn't feel that your choice is capable of carrying out the responsibilities of the job or if your heirs formally object to your choice and the court upholds their objections.

As you know from reading Chapter 1, only those assets in your estate that pass under your will go through probate. These assets include

- all assets you own in your own name;
- your share of any assets you own as a tenant in common;

- half of your community property, depending on your state;
- life insurance death benefits when your estate is the beneficiary; and
- property placed in a testamentary trust.

See Figure 6.1 for a list of the assets that do not go through probate.

John D. Rockefeller, Sr., founder of Standard Oil Company, gave away $531 million during his lifetime for educational, religious and charitable purposes. See Figure 6.2 for his net estate table.

Potential Drawbacks of Probate

Many negatives are commonly associated with the traditional, formal probate process. People complain that it's too expensive, that it's

FIGURE 6.1

Assets That Are Not Probated

Not all of the assets in your estate will be probated. Therefore, one strategy for reducing the time your estate is tied up in the probate process is to maximize the assets you own that will not be probated. These assets include

- jointly owned property—that is, property held as joint tenants with right of survivorship or as tenants by the entirety;

- *inter vivos* gifts;

- assets placed in payable-on-death or trust accounts;

- death benefits from IRAs, life insurance policies and retirement plans, as long as your estate is not their beneficiary;

- property placed in living trusts;

- some business property controlled by contracts; and

- depending on your state, community property that goes to a spouse.

FIGURE 6.2

John D. Rockefeller, Sr.: Net Estate Table
Founder, Standard Oil Co., Industrialist and Philanthropist,
Pocantico Hills, Tarrytown, New York

GROSS ESTATE	**$26,905,182**
Debts	*$133,348*
Administrative Expenses	*85,996*
Attorney Fees	*200,000*
Executor Fees	*75,000*
N.Y. Inheritance Tax	*4,385,644*
*Fed. Estate Tax**	*12,245,000*
TOTAL COSTS	**$17,124,988**
CASH IN ESTATE	**$1,705,488**
NET ESTATE	**$9,780,194**

*No marital deduction

excessively time consuming for an executor and that it creates needless delays in the transfer of property to a deceased person's beneficiaries. Some people also object to probate's public nature because the details of a will as well as the list of all the assets in an estate are available to anyone interested.

The length of the formal probate process can vary widely, but typically it takes six months to a year for the process to be completed. However, its duration can be affected by many factors, including

- the amount of assets in your probate estate and the complexity of those assets;
- the number of beneficiaries named in your will;
- whether anyone contests the validity of your will or challenges one of its provisions;
- the number of creditor claims against your estate;

- the probate laws of your state;
- the efficiency of the particular court supervising the probate process for your estate;
- whether your estate must file an estate tax return (If it does, it can be two to three years before everything is resolved with the IRS.);
- whether it takes time to locate your will;
- whether a self-proving affidavit exists if the witnesses to the signing of your will can't be found or are no longer alive; and
- how time consuming or complicated it is to locate and appraise the assets in your estate.

The Costs of Probate

The expenses of the formal probate process can eat up as much as 10 percent of an estate, according to the American Association of Retired Persons (AARP). Those expenses can include court costs, appraisal costs, fiduciary fees (fees paid to your executor) and attorney fees.

You can do a number of things to minimize probate expenses. For example, thoroughly planning your estate and writing a good will decrease the likelihood that problems will develop that would cost your estate money. Also, selecting an executor willing and able to do much of the work that an attorney would otherwise do during probate can also save you money. This may be possible if your estate is very simple and the probate process is trouble-free because much of the work involved in probate is gathering information and filling out forms. However, in reality, nearly every executor uses an attorney for at least some aspect of the probate process. Because an attorney can often save an executor time and money, not using one is usually a matter of being penny-wise and pound-foolish.

 **HOT TIP**

A nice clean estate with no tax liability pays about $1,000 in probate-related attorney fees and court costs.

Your estate can also save on probate-related costs if you pass as much of it as possible over or outside your will rather than under it. This strategy can be especially cost effective if your state determines probate fees based on the value of an estate.

Court Costs

In most states, court costs are relatively insignificant, usually only a few hundred dollars at the most. Although the court costs your estate must pay depend on the requirements of your state, they can include filing fees, registration fees, publication fees and fees based on the value of your probate estate.

Appraisal Costs

Appraisal costs cover the process of determining the value of property in your probate estate, aside from cash, publicly traded securities and similar assets. This determination is usually done by an appraiser. In a modest estate, appraisal costs can range from a couple of hundred dollars to a few thousand, depending on the amount and types of assets.

Fiduciary Fees

Fiduciary fees are the fees paid to your executor or to a state-appointed administrator. States limit the amount an executor may receive, and an executor's fees must be approved by the probate court before they can be paid. As mentioned in Chapter 1, family members and close friends who serve as executors often waive the payment of fiduciary fees.

Fiduciary fees are calculated as a percentage of the net value of an estate or are determined on the basis of "reasonableness" as defined by a state. If the fees are calculated as a percentage of net value, they will be based on the total appraised value of all the property in your estate less the total amount of debt secured by that property.

Compare the executor's fee of $5 million described in Doris Duke's will to what the executor of Henry Kaiser, Jr.'s estate received. (See Figure 6.3.)

FIGURE 6.3

Henry J. Kaiser, Jr.: Net Estate Table
Executive Vice President, Kaiser Industries, Oakland,
California

GROSS ESTATE* **$55,910,373**

Debts	*$61,716*
Administrative Expenses	*27,989*
Attorney Fees	*18,860*
Executor Fees	*None*
Calif. Inheritance Tax	*149,398*
*Fed. Estate Tax***	*772,452*

TOTAL COSTS **$1,030,415**

CASH IN ESTATE **$27,898**

NET ESTATE **$54,879,958**

---

*Included in the gross estate is $375,000 of life insurance. Stock in certain corporations was transferred before death into a trust (all separate property), which, after death, was charged with paying all taxes, allowances and claims of the decedent, and a balance to Kaiser Family Foundation, a charitable organization.

**$27,891,473 marital deduction

Attorney Fees

As already indicated, most executors need the services of an attorney to help them through the probate process. Attorneys typically charge for their services on an hourly basis.

Potential Benefits of Probate

Traditionally, people have focused on the drawbacks of probate and, therefore, on how to avoid the process. However, it is important not to overlook two benefits to probate. First, probate helps ensure

> ### ✎ HOT TIP
>
> ———————————————————
>
> If an attorney proposes charging for his or her services by taking a percentage of an estate's value, the executor should find another attorney. This is not the way most reputable estate attorneys charge these days.

that only those individuals or organizations with true claims to your estate will get your property after you die. Second, probate limits the amount of time that creditors with claims against your estate can try to get paid. This period usually runs between four and six months. Credi-

FIGURE 6.4

William Randolph Hearst: Net Estate Table
Publisher, Los Angeles, California

———————————————————

GROSS ESTATE*	**$57,115,167**
Debts	*$481,945*
Administrative Expenses	*136,287*
Attorney Fees	*748,936*
Executor Fees	*663,436*
Calif. Inheritance Tax	*618,930*
*Fed. Estate Tax**	*1,078,812*
TOTAL COSTS	**$3,728,346**
CASH IN ESTATE	**$206,500**
NET ESTATE	**$53,386,821**

*Approximately 75 percent of estate went to William Randolph Hearst Foundation. Property valued at $472,200 was given to Marion Davies Douras.

**$5,446,516 marital deduction

tors that don't present their claims within this time period cannot pursue their collection efforts.

How the Formal Probate Process Works

The formal probate process varies from state to state. However, the summary that follows is a good overview of the steps typically involved.

Step 1. After you die, any of your heirs, beneficiaries or creditors can initiate the probate process by filing a *petition for probate* with the probate court in the county of residence.

Step 2. Once a petition is filed, the court either appoints the executor you've named in your will or appoints an administrator. The court also makes sure that your will is legally valid.

Step 3. Depending on your state, your executor may have to notify all your potential heirs as well as all your potential creditors that probate has begun. They will have a set amount of time—usually several months—to file claims against your estate. If one of your legal heirs is not included in your will or is unhappy with what you left him or her, the heir might file a claim. Also, an heir might contest your will if he or she questions your mental competency at the time you wrote your will. See Figure 6.5 for a list of the grounds that can be used to contest a will.

If no claims are filed and no one contests the validity of your will, the court formally approves it and admits it to probate.

Step 4. Your executor prepares and files a final list of the assets in your probate estate, files tax returns if necessary and begins preparations to transfer probate property to your beneficiaries according to the instructions in your will.

Step 5. Any creditor, including tax entities, that filed a legitimate claim within the required period of time is paid by your estate. If your executor contests the validity or amount of a claim, this step may take considerable time to complete.

FIGURE 6.5

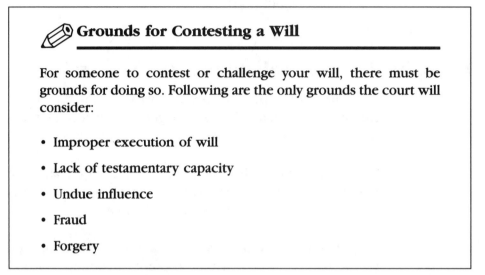

✏ Grounds for Contesting a Will

For someone to contest or challenge your will, there must be grounds for doing so. Following are the only grounds the court will consider:

- Improper execution of will

- Lack of testamentary capacity

- Undue influence

- Fraud

- Forgery

Step 6. Your executor completes all final paperwork, prepares a final report for the court and petitions the court to close your estate. This won't happen until all necessary fees and expenses have been paid and any estate-related issues have been resolved. Your legal heirs can contest the executor's final accounting. If they do, the court holds a hearing.

Step 7. The probate judge formally closes your estate and releases your executor from any further duties.

The Family Allowance

Most states allow a surviving spouse and dependent children to receive a *family allowance* while the deceased's estate is probated. The allowance helps ensure that a family does not suffer financially during this time. The family allowance will be paid by the estate and will come to the spouse and dependent children in addition to any property and income they are due to receive. If your state is a separate property state, the spouse can receive the family allowance as well as the state's elective share.

States vary in regard to how they calculate the amount of a family allowance. Some use a set amount that doesn't vary by family size or other factors. Others consider a number of variables when determining the appropriate amount of a family allowance, including the overall financial status of a surviving spouse and the number of dependent children he or she has to raise.

Some states also protect a surviving spouse and minor children from losing their homestead to creditors. In addition, these states prohibit the heirs or beneficiaries of the deceased spouse from forcing the surviving spouse to move out of the homestead, even if the homestead has been left to the deceased's heirs or beneficiaries in full or in part.

Alternatives to the Formal Probate Process

Most states provide alternatives to the formal probate process for estates that are limited in size and complexity and that have few beneficiaries, few creditors and no estate or inheritance tax liabilities. The benefit of these alternatives is that they require little if any involvement of the probate court and, therefore, are quicker and cheaper than the formal process. Although these alternatives vary among states, two of the more common are summary administration and collection by affidavit. Their general eligibility requirements and applicable restrictions, as well as an overview of the way each works, are described below.

Summary Administration

Eligible estates. Any estate that has an executor, whose value is less than a state-set maximum—usually $50,000 or less—and that meets other state criteria is eligible.

How it works. The executor immediately transfers assets in the will to the appropriate beneficiaries and files a formal accounting with the court. Intermediate steps such as the notification of creditors, the waiting period for creditors and the formal inventory and appraisal are eliminated.

Restrictions. The consent of all beneficiaries to a will may have to be obtained for summary administration to be used.

Collection by Affidavit

Eligible estates. Any estate whose net value is less than an amount set by the state is eligible.

How it works. Anyone who believes that he or she is entitled to certain personal property of the deceased may complete an affidavit to that effect, and the holder of the property can transfer it to the person who completed the affidavit.

Restrictions. Restrictions vary by state, but some states allow only spouses and children to collect by affidavit; some states allow only certain types of property to be collected by affidavit; and some states require a minimal amount of court involvement.

Avoiding Probate

Although many people want to avoid probate, it's hard to do. Even with the best estate planning, it's easy to overlook an asset, and that oversight may require your estate to go through probate. Many other people do not want to avoid probate completely but do want to minimize the number and value of assets that must go through probate. Still others want to plan their estates so they qualify for the less formal probate processes described in the previous sections. You can accomplish any of these goals by

- owning as many assets as possible as a joint tenant with right of survivorship;
- owning assets with your spouse as a tenant by the entirety;
- making someone the beneficiary of your life insurance policy, employee benefits plan or IRA;
- making *inter vivos* gifts to your beneficiaries;
- setting up payable-on-death or trust accounts; or
- setting up living trusts.

The role of probate in your estate is something to discuss with your attorney. To prepare for that discussion, you may want to return to Chapters 1 and 4, which discussed in detail the probate avoidance and minimization options outlined previously.

Taxes and Your Estate

When you die, your estate may have to pay taxes. The more taxes it must pay, the less will remain for your beneficiaries. Therefore, an important part of estate planning for many people, especially those with substantial estates, involves tax minimization. Following are some of the taxes your estate may have to pay.

Estate income tax. Your estate must pay this tax if the income it earns in any tax year exceeds the standard exemptions an estate receives.

Federal estate tax. Your estate must pay this graduated tax only if the estate's value exceeds a certain dollar limit—$600,000 if you're single and $1.2 million if you're married. Its value is based on the current fair market value of all the assets in your estate, not just those that go through probate. The total value also includes the cumulative amount of any *inter vivos* gifts you have made. Every dollar exceeding the $600,000 and $1.2 million limits will be taxed at 37 percent to 55 percent.

State estate tax. Your estate may be liable to pay estate taxes to your state as well as to the federal government.

Personal income tax. This is the tax due on your income in the year of your death.

Appendix B includes examples of some of the IRS forms that may have to be filed for your estate after you die.

The Unlimited Marital Tax Deduction

The unlimited marital tax deduction gives married people a break on their federal estate taxes. It allows one spouse to leave all or a portion of his or her estate, regardless of its value, to the other spouse without incurring any tax liability.

✎ HOT TIP

The unlimited marital deduction is not available to noncitizen spouses except through a qualified domestic trust.

Although this deduction provides an undeniable immediate benefit to your surviving spouse, without the right estate planning, it can create future tax problems for your spouse's estate. This is because use of the tax deduction only postpones payment of the estate taxes; they will have to be paid by your surviving spouse's estate when he or she dies. Furthermore, if your surviving spouse owns assets in his or her own name, and if the assets you leave your spouse appreciate subsequently, your spouse's estate may face a tax liability even greater than yours. Therefore, given the potential drawbacks of using the unlimited marital tax deduction, consult an estate attorney if you feel that the deduction may create future tax problems for your spouse. You might need to set up a trust to avoid potential problems.

State Taxes

Some states have their own estate taxes. Often, they impose their taxes on estates valued at less than $600,000, which means that even modest estates may need to be concerned about state estate taxes. However, the state rate is much lower than the federal government's rate.

Strategies To Reduce Your Estate Taxes

If it appears that your estate will owe taxes, you can take action to reduce or even wipe out that liability. The right options for you should be determined by you and your attorney as part of your overall estate plan. See Figure 6.6 for five ways to reduce your estate taxes.

FIGURE 6.6

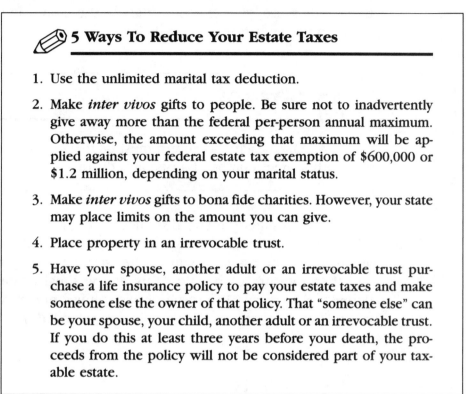

✐ 5 Ways To Reduce Your Estate Taxes

1. Use the unlimited marital tax deduction.

2. Make *inter vivos* gifts to people. Be sure not to inadvertently give away more than the federal per-person annual maximum. Otherwise, the amount exceeding that maximum will be applied against your federal estate tax exemption of $600,000 or $1.2 million, depending on your marital status.

3. Make *inter vivos* gifts to bona fide charities. However, your state may place limits on the amount you can give.

4. Place property in an irrevocable trust.

5. Have your spouse, another adult or an irrevocable trust purchase a life insurance policy to pay your estate taxes and make someone else the owner of that policy. That "someone else" can be your spouse, your child, another adult or an irrevocable trust. If you do this at least three years before your death, the proceeds from the policy will not be considered part of your taxable estate.

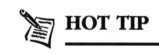 **HOT TIP**

The person to whom you give the policy must make the payments on it, not you. Otherwise, you'll be considered the policy owner and you won't realize any tax benefits.

If Your Estate Must Pay Taxes

If your estate owes taxes, they must be paid before your beneficiaries can receive what you have left them. If you made special provisions in your will for paying your taxes, your executor will follow them. Otherwise, your executor will use the money in your residuary estate to pay your taxes.

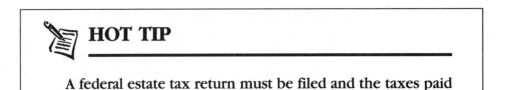

HOT TIP

A federal estate tax return must be filed and the taxes paid within nine months of a person's death.

If your residuary estate does not have enough money to pay all of the taxes your estate owes, payment of taxes will be apportioned among all of the assets in your estate, starting with general bequests and then moving to specific bequests; personal property is tapped before real property. As a result of this apportionment, your beneficiaries will end up with less than what you intended them to receive.

HOT TIP

Unless all estate-related taxes are paid to the IRS, that agency will use any of the collection tools available to it. Those tools include seizing assets and levying bank accounts. (See Figure 6.7.)

FIGURE 6.7

Robert S. Kerr: Net Estate Table
U.S. Senator, Oklahoma, Oklahoma City, Oklahoma

GROSS ESTATE **$20,800,000**

Debts	*$ (Unknown)*
Administrative Expenses	*(Borne by heirs)*
Attorney Fees	*220,000*
Executor Fees	*220,000*
Okla. Estate Tax and Fed. Tax*	*9,400,000*

TOTAL COSTS **$9,840,000**

CASH IN ESTATE **$113,000**

NET ESTATE **$10,960,000**

---

*33⅓ percent marital deduction

Under the will, the widow was given a life estate in one-sixth of the estate left for her in trust. She renounced the will and chose to take as a forced heir, as if the decedent died intestate, all as provided by Oklahoma law, thereby commanding one-third of the entire estate.

The executors petitioned the probate court for permission to borrow $6.1 million from two banks to help pay estate taxes rather than sell shares of Kerr-McGee Oil Industries, Inc., stock (449,882 shares valued at $14,472,703), which would have depressed the market and caused substantial loss to the estate. The exact gross estate has not been determined, owing to the complexity of valuations.

CHAPTER
SEVEN

Sample Wills

This chapter will feature a number of sample wills. Their purpose, together with the celebrity wills in Appendix A and the commentary on those celebrity wills running throughout this book, is to illustrate the general format and typical wording of various types of wills as well as the kinds of provisions a will can include.

The chapter will also present a number of different clauses that address specific situations that may apply to you. In addition, it will include a sample self-proving affidavit.

Explanations for and Limitations of Sample Wills

There is no set way that a will must be worded; however, certain terms and phrases have become matters of convention. Also, precise, un-ambiguous words are always best so that no question exists regarding the intent of a particular sentence or clause. The wills in this chapter as well as in Appendix A will help accustom you to the typical language

If you read the wills of famous people included in Appendix A, you'll notice varying lengths. Sometimes the length of a will reflects good estate planning; sometimes not.

Everyone who makes a will has different concerns, different goals. That's why a standard fill-in-the-blanks will is usually not appropriate for most people. It doesn't give you the flexibility to do exactly what you want or need to do. Also, a fill-in-the blanks will may be defective in some way, possibly creating delays during the probate process or completely invalidating the will.

used in wills. However, whenever possible, unnecessary legalese has been eliminated from them.

One note of caution regarding the sample wills in this chapter: Don't assume that if you find one that fits your general circumstances, you can use it as the basis for creating your own will. Although you may be well served by writing your own will based on one of the wills in this chapter, as this book has already emphasized, you should get the help of an attorney to draft a will that meets your particular estate planning goals and concerns and that meets the specific requirements of your state. Also, as indicated, without an attorney's help, you may not be aware of things you should address in your will or things you should deal with using estate planning tools in addition to a will.

When appropriate, italicized explanations follow selected clauses in the sample wills. Please note, however, that an explanation appears only the first time a clause is used; the explanation is not repeated in subsequent wills.

Sample Will for a Single Person with Minor Children

With an estimated 50 percent of all American marriages ending in divorce, this type of will applies to a growing number of people.

Last Will and Testament
of
(Your name)

Clause 1

I, *(Your name)*, a resident
in *(Your city and state of residence)*, being of sound mind and not
acting under any duress, fraud or undue influence of any person, declare
this instrument as my LAST WILL AND TESTAMENT.

*If you own property in a name different from the one you use in this
will, or if you changed your name and use that new name in your
will, insert the following phrase into the clause above:*
I, *(Your name)*, also known as *(Other name/s)* . . .
Be sure to share your other name (or names) with your attorney.

A good example of a person who used other names and included
them in his will is Liberace. Look at his will in Appendix A, and you will
see it begins, "I, Liberace, also sometimes known as Walter Valentino
Liberace, Lee Liberace and Wladsiv Valentino Liberace, domiciled in
Las Vegas, Nevada, being of sound mind and memory, do hereby make,
publish and declare this to be my Last Will and Testament, and hereby
revoke any and all wills and codicils at any time heretofore made by
me."

Clause 2: Revocation

I hereby revoke all prior wills and codicils by me.
*Even if you have no recollection of ever having written a will, in-
clude this clause in your will. It's a matter of being on the safe side,
just in case your memory is poor.*

Clause 3: Identification of Family

I am presently unmarried. I am the *(Mother or father)* of the follow-
ing children, all living at the time this will was written and executed:
(Name of child)   *(Date of birth)*
(Name of child)   *(Date of birth)*
*If you were previously married, add a paragraph that states the
name of your former spouse(s) and why the marriage(s) ended:*
I was formerly married to *(Name of former spouse)*. This marriage
ended by *(Specify divorce, annulment or death)*.

Clause 4: Appointment of Executor

I appoint *(Name of executor)* as executor of this will. If *(He/she)* cannot or will not serve in this capacity, I appoint *(Name of substitute executor)* as my substitute executor. *You can also name coexecutors.* In addition to all the powers allowable under the laws of this state, I authorize and empower my executor to *(Itemize all of the additional powers and responsibilities you give your executor.)*

I request that my executor be allowed to act without having to post any bond or other kind of security.

Typical additional powers and responsibilities you can give to your executor include

- *the freedom to retain the property in your estate without liability for its depreciation or loss;*
- *the ability to sell, lease or exchange, by public or private means, real or personal property and to administer any proceeds as appropriate;*
- *the freedom to exercise all of the rights of a person who owns securities;*
- *the freedom to pay all legal claims against your estate, including any debts you owed at the time of your death and any estate taxes that may arise from your death, provided that such debts and taxes are paid first from your residuary estate;*
- *the right to operate, sell, encumber, maintain or dispose of any business or part of a business that is in your estate;*
- *the right to distribute property to the guardian, custodian or trustee for the benefit of any minor children you have;*
- *the freedom to defend or settle any claims for or against your estate; and*
- *the right to take all other actions that your executor feels are necessary and appropriate for the proper management, investment and distribution of your estate.*

Elvis Presley's will shows he made his father executor of his estate and trustee of his trusts. If you go through the wills in Appendix A, you will see the range of powers the executors were given.

Clause 5: Appointment of Guardian

In the event I shall die leaving any of my children as minors and my former spouse does not survive me, I appoint as personal and property guardian of my minor children *(Name of guardian)*. If *(He/she)* dies, resigns or is otherwise unable to serve as personal and property guardian, I appoint *(Name of alternate guardian)* as successor guardian.

The guardian shall serve without bond or surety and without the intervention of any court except as required by law.

You can name a different guardian for each child if that makes practical sense. You can also name different people to serve as personal and property guardians.

Jerry Garcia appointed Sunshine May Walker Kesey as the guardian of Keelin Garcia, his minor daughter, if her mother did not survive him.

Clause 6: Disposition of Property

I give all of my estate to my children to be divided among them in equal shares. If one of my children shall not survive me by 30 days, the surviving child should receive all of the aforementioned gift. If neither child survives me by 30 days, my estate is to be distributed as follows:

I give *(Name of beneficiary)* my *(Description of property)*, if *(He/she)* survives me by 60 days. If *(He/she)* does not survive me, I give the above-described property to *(Name of alternate beneficiary)*, if *(He/she)* survives me. If neither of the above persons survives me, the above-described property should be disposed of with the residue of my estate.

Repeat the above clause if necessary.

I give the sum of $*(Dollar amount)* to *(Name of beneficiary)*, if *(He/she)* survives me by 60 days. If *(He/she)* does not survive me, I give the same sum of money to *(Name of alternate beneficiary)*, if *(He/she)* survives me. If neither of the above persons survives me, this same sum of money should be disposed of with the residue of my estate.

Repeat the above clause if necessary.

Clause 7: Residuary Estate

I give the rest of my estate, all the property I own that is not legally disposed of by this will or in some other manner, to *(Name of residual beneficiary)*. In the event *(He/she)* does not survive me by 60 days, I give the aforementioned gift to *(Name of alternate beneficiary)*.

If any primary beneficiary of a shared residuary or specific gift made by me in this will fails to survive me by 60 days, the surviving beneficiaries of that gift shall equally divide between them the deceased beneficiary's share. If all primary beneficiaries of a shared residuary or specific gift fail to survive me by 60 days, that gift shall pass to the alternate beneficiaries named to receive that gift. If the alternate beneficiaries named in this will to receive a specific gift fail to survive me by 60 days, or no such named alternate beneficiaries exist, that gift shall become part of my residuary estate.

If you look at Henry Fonda's will in Appendix A, the residuary clause leaves his estate to the Omaha Community Playhouse if his wife does not survive him by 90 days.

Clause 8: Signature

I subscribe my name to this will on the *(Date)* day of *(Month)*, 19 *(Year)*, at *(City, county and state)*, and declare that I am a legal and competent adult and that I did not enter into or sign this will under duress, constraint or undue influence.

(Your legal signature)

Clause 9: Attestation

On this *(Date)* day of *(Month)*, 19 *(Year)*, *(Your name)* declared to us, the undersigned, that this document was *(His/her)* will and asked us to serve as witnesses, signing our names accordingly. At the request of *(Your name)*, and in *(His/her)* presence, and in the presence of each other, all being present at the same time, we have signed our names as witnesses. We declare this to be the will of *(Your name)*, and that to the best of our knowledge, *(Your name)* is a competent adult and was under no undue influence, duress or constraint at the time of this signing. Under penalty of perjury, we declare that the foregoing is true and correct.

(Witness's signature)
(Witness's address)

(Witness's signature)
(Witness's address)

(Witness's signature)
(Witness's address)

Sample Will for a Single Person with No Children

This is an example of a basic will that might be appropriate for young people just starting their careers and in the early stages of building their wealth.

Last Will and Testament
of
(Your name)

Clause 1

I, *(Your name)*, a resident in *(Your city and state of residence)*, being of sound mind and not acting under any duress, fraud or undue influence of any person, declare this instrument as my LAST WILL AND TESTAMENT.

Clause 2: Revocation

I hereby revoke all prior wills and codicils by me.

Clause 3: Identification of Family

I am presently unmarried and have no living children.
I have never been formerly married.
If you've never been married, this clause is not necessary, but including it leaves nothing to question.

Clause 4: Appointment of Executor

I appoint *(Name of executor)* as executor of this will. If *(He/she)* cannot or will not serve in this capacity, I appoint *(Name of substitute executor)* as my substitute executor. In addition to all of the powers allowable under the laws of this state, I authorize and empower my executor to *(Itemize all of the additional powers and responsibilities you give your executor.)*
I request that my executor be allowed to act without having to post any bond or other kind of security.

Clause 5: Disposition of Property

I give *(Name of beneficiary)* my *(Description of property)*, if *(He/she)* survives me by 30 days. If *(He/she)* does not survive me by 30 days, I give the above-described property to *(Name of alternate beneficiary)*, if *(He/she)* survives me by 30 days. If neither of the above persons survives me by 30 days, the above-described property should be disposed of with the residue of my estate.

Repeat the above clause if necessary.

Clause 6: Residuary Estate

I give the rest of my estate, all the property I own that is not legally disposed of by this will or in some other manner, to *(Name of residual beneficiary)*. In the event *(He/she)* does not survive me by 30 days, I give my residuary estate to *(Name of charity)* at *(Address of charity)* for the general support of its activities.

Clause 7: Signature

I subscribe my name to this will on the *(Date)* day of *(Month)*, 19 *(Year)*, at *(City, county and state)*, and declare that I am a legal and competent adult and that I did not enter into or sign this will under duress, constraint or undue influence.

(Your legal signature)

Clause 8: Attestation

On this *(Date)* day of *(Month)*, 19 *(Year)*, *(Your name)* declared to us, the undersigned, that this document was *(His/her)* will and asked us to serve as witnesses, signing our names accordingly. At the request of *(Your name)*, and in *(His/her)* presence, and in the presence of each other, all being present at the same time, we have signed our names as witnesses. We declare this to be the will of *(Your name)*, and that to the best of our knowledge, *(Your name)* is a competent adult and was under no undue influence, duress or constraint at the time of this signing. Under penalty of perjury, we declare that the foregoing is true and correct.

(Witness's signature)
(Witness's address)

(Witness's signature)
(Witness's address)

(Witness's signature)
(Witness's address)

Sample Will for a Married Person with Minor Children

As this book has already indicated, parents of minor children have special issues to consider when doing estate planning. The following will is a very simple example of how some parents might address these issues. Trusts and custodianships are two other possible estate planning tools to help parents provide for minor children.

Last Will and Testament
of
(Your name)

Clause 1

I, *(Your name)*, a resident in *(Your city and state of residence)*, being of sound mind and not acting under any duress, fraud or undue influence of any person, declare this instrument as my LAST WILL AND TESTAMENT.

Clause 2: Revocation

I hereby revoke all prior wills and codicils by me.

Clause 3: Identification of Family

My spouse's name is *(Name of spouse)*. All references in this will to *(Him/her)* or to my spouse shall refer only to *(Name of spouse)*.

I have not been married previously.

I am the *(Mother/father)* of the following children, all living at the time this will was written and executed:

(Name of child)	*(Date of birth)*
(Name of child)	*(Date of birth)*

Clause 4: Appointment of Executor

I appoint *(Name of executor)* as executor of this will. If *(He/she)* cannot or will not serve in this capacity, I appoint *(Name of substitute executor)* as my substitute executor. In addition to all of the powers allowable under the laws of this state, I authorize and empower my executor to *(Itemize all of the additional powers and responsibilities you give your executor.)*.

I request that my executor be allowed to act without having to post any bond or other kind of security.

Clause 5: Appointment of Guardian

In the event I shall die leaving any of my children as minors and my spouse does not survive me, I appoint as personal and property guardian of my minor children *(Name of guardian)*. If *(He/she)* dies, resigns or is otherwise unable to serve as personal and property guardian, I appoint *(Name of alternate guardian)* as successor guardian.

The guardian shall serve without bond or surety and without the intervention of any court except as required by law.

Clause 6: Disposition of Property

I give all of my property to my spouse, *(Spouse's full name)*. If *(He/she)* does not survive me by 30 days, I give that property to my children who survive me, to be divided equally among them by my executor.

Although most married people leave all of their property to their surviving spouses, you can divide your property any way you want. Therefore, you can designate specific beneficiaries to receive specific assets. Also, you can organize your gift giving into categories such as cash, personal property and real property, as the previous sample will did.

Chief Justice Warren Burger gave one-third of his estate to his daughter, Margaret Elizabeth Burger Rose, and two-thirds to his son, Wade A. Burger.

Clause 7: Residuary Estate

I give the rest of my estate, all the property I own that is not legally disposed of by this will or in some other manner, to *(Name of residual beneficiary)*. In the event *(He/she)* does not survive me by 30 days, I give the aforementioned gift to *(Name of alternate beneficiary)*.

If any primary beneficiary of a shared residuary or specific gift made by me in this will fails to survive me by 30 days, the surviving beneficiaries of that gift shall equally divide between them the deceased beneficiary's share. If all primary beneficiaries of a shared residuary or specific gift fail to survive me by 30 days, that gift shall pass to the alternate beneficiaries named to receive that gift. If the alternate beneficiaries named in this will to receive a specific gift fail to survive me by 30 days, or no such named alternate beneficiaries exist, that gift shall become part of my residuary estate.

Clause 8: Simultaneous Death and Survivorship

If I and *(Name of spouse)* die at the same time or under such circumstances that it is difficult or impossible to ascertain which of us died first, my spouse shall be deemed to have predeceased me. No person other than my spouse shall be deemed to have survived me if such person dies within 30 days after me.

Clause 9: Signature

I subscribe my name to this will on the *(Date)* day of *(Month)*, 19 *(Year)*, at *(City, county and state)*, and declare that I am a legal and competent adult and that I did not enter into or sign this will under duress, constraint or undue influence.

(Your legal signature)

Clause 10: Attestation

On this *(Date)* day of *(Month)*, 19 *(Year)*, *(Your name)* declared to us, the undersigned, that this document was *(His/her)* will and asked us to serve as witnesses, signing our names accordingly. At the request of *(Your name)*, and in *(His/her)* presence, and in the presence of each other, all being present at the same time, we have signed our names as witnesses. We declare this to be the will of *(Your name)*, and that to the best of our knowledge, *(Your name)* is a competent adult and was under no undue influence, duress or constraint at the time of this signing. Under penalty of perjury, we declare that the foregoing is true and correct.

(Witness's signature)
(Witness's address)

(Witness's signature)
(Witness's address)

(Witness's signature)
(Witness's address)

Sample Will for a Married Person with No Children

Childless married people may leave relatively more of their estates to nieces and nephews, friends and charities than would married people concerned about leaving property to their children.

Last Will and Testament
of
(Your name)

Clause 1

I, *(Your name)*, a resident in *(Your city and state of residence)*, being of sound mind and not acting under any duress, fraud or undue influence of any person, declare this instrument as my LAST WILL AND TESTAMENT.

Clause 2: Revocation

I hereby revoke all prior wills and codicils by me.

Clause 3: Identification of Family

My spouse's name is *(Name of spouse)*. All references in this will to *(Him/her)* or to my spouse shall refer only to *(Name of spouse)*.

I was formerly married to *(Name of former spouse)*. That marriage ended by *(Specify divorce, annulment or death)*.

Clause 4: Appointment of Executor

I appoint *(Name of executor)* as executor of this will. If *(He/she)* cannot or will not serve in this capacity, I appoint *(Name of substitute executor)* as my substitute executor. In addition to all of the powers allowable under the laws of this state, I authorize and empower my executor to *(Itemize all the additional powers and responsibilities you give your executor.)*.

I request that my executor be allowed to act without having to post any bond or other kind of security.

Clause 5: Disposition of Property

I give all of my property to my spouse, *(Spouse's name)*, if *(He/she)* survives me by 30 days. If *(He/she)* does not survive me by 30 days, I distribute all of my property as follows:

I give *(Name of beneficiary)*, my *(Description of property)*, if *(He/she)* survives me by 30 days. If *(He/she)* does not survive me by 30 days, I give the above-described property to *(Name of alternate beneficiary)*, if *(He/she)* survives me. If neither of the above persons survives me by 30 days, the above-described property should be disposed of with the residue of my estate.

Repeat the above clause if necessary.

I give the sum of $*(Dollar amount)* to *(Name of beneficiary)*, if *(He/she)* survives me by 30 days. If *(He/she)* does not survive me by 30 days, I give the same sum of money to *(Name of alternate beneficiary)*, if *(He/she)* survives me. If neither of the above persons survives me by 30 days, the above-described property should be disposed of with the residue of my estate.

Repeat the above clause if necessary.

I give my *(Description of real estate item)* at *(Street address, city, county and state)* to *(Name of beneficiary)*, if *(He/she)* survives me by 30 days. If *(He/she)* does not survive me by 30 days, I give the above-described property to *(Name of alternate beneficiary)*, if *(He/she)* survives me. If neither of the above persons survives me by 30 days, the above-described property should be disposed of with the residue of my estate.

Repeat the above clause as necessary.

Clause 6: Residuary Estate

I give the rest of my estate, all the property I own that is not legally disposed of by this will or in some other manner, to *(Name of residual beneficiary)*. In the event *(He/she)* does not survive me by 30 days, I give my residuary estate to *(Name of alternate beneficary)*.

If any primary beneficiary of a shared residuary or specific gift made by me in this will fails to survive me by 30 days, the surviving beneficiaries of that gift shall equally divide between them the deceased beneficiary's share. If all primary beneficiaries of a shared residuary or specific gift fail to survive me by 30 days, that gift shall pass to the alternate beneficiaries named to receive that gift. If the alternate beneficiaries named in this will to receive a specific gift fail to survive me by 30 days, or no such named alternate beneficiaries exist, that gift shall become part of my residuary estate.

Clause 7: Simultaneous Death and Survivorship

If I and *(Name of spouse)* die at the same time or under such circumstances that it is difficult or impossible to ascertain which of us died first, my spouse shall be deemed to have predeceased me. No person other than my spouse shall be deemed to have survived me if such person dies within 30 days after me.

This same clause should be in your spouse's will. That way, each will can be probated according to the estate plans you've both set up.

Clause 8: Signature

I subscribe my name to this will on the *(Date)* day of *(Month)*, 19 *(Year)*, at *(City, county and state)*, and declare that I am a legal and competent adult and that I did not enter into or sign this will under duress, constraint or undue influence.

(Your legal signature)

Clause 9: Attestation

On this *(Date)* day of *(Month)*, 19 *(Year)*, *(Your name)* declared to us, the undersigned, that this document was *(His/her)* will and asked us to serve as witnesses, signing our names accordingly. At the request of *(Your name)*, and in *(His/her)* presence, and in the presence of each other, all being present at the same time, we have signed our names as witnesses. We declare this to be the will of *(Your name)*, and that to the best of our knowledge, *(Your name)* is a competent adult and was under no undue influence, duress or constraint at the time of this signing. Under penalty of perjury, we declare that the foregoing is true and correct.

(Witness's signature)
(Witness's address)

(Witness's signature)
(Witness's address)

(Witness's signature)
(Witness's address)

Sample Will for an Unmarried Person with Minor Children Who Lives with a Partner

This will is very similar to the one for a married person with young children. However, this particular will includes provisions for using the Uniform Gifts or Transfers to Minors Act.

Last Will and Testament
of
(Your name)

Clause 1

I, *(Your name)*, a resident in *(Your city and state of residence)*, being of sound mind and not acting under any duress, fraud or undue influence of any person, declare this instrument as my LAST WILL AND TESTAMENT.

Clause 2: Revocation

I hereby revoke all prior wills and codicils by me.

Clause 3: Identification of Family

I am presently unmarried. I am the *(Mother/father)* of the following children, all living at the time this will was written and executed.
(Name of child)   *(Date of birth)*
(Name of child)   *(Date of birth)*
I was formerly married to *(Name of former spouse)*. This marriage ended by *(Specify divorce, annulment or death)*.
The name of my partner is *(Name of partner)*, and all references in this will to my partner are to *(Him/her)*.

Clause 4: Appointment of Executor

I appoint *(Name of executor)* as executor of this will. If *(He/she)* cannot or will not serve in this capacity, I appoint *(Name of substitute executor)* as my substitute executor. In addition to all of the powers allowable under the laws of this state, I authorize and empower my executor to *(Itemize all of the additional powers and responsibilities you give your executor.)*.
I request that my executor be allowed to act without having to post any bond or other kind of security.

Clause 5: Appointment of Guardian

In the event I shall die leaving any of my children as minors, I appoint as personal and property guardian of my minor children *(Name of guardian)*. If *(He/she)* dies, resigns or is otherwise unable to serve as personal and property guardian, I appoint *(Name of alternate guardian)* as successor guardian.

The guardian shall serve without bond or surety and without the intervention of any court except as required by law.

Clause 6: Disposition of Property

I give *(Name of beneficiary)* my *(Description of property)*, if *(He/she)* survives me by 30 days. If *(He/she)* does not survive me by 30 days, I give the above-described property to *(Name of alternate beneficiary)*, if *(He/she)* survives me by 30 days. If neither of the above persons survives me, the above-described property should be disposed of with the residue of my estate.

Repeat the above clause as necessary.

I give the sum of $*(Dollar amount)* to *(Name of beneficiary)*, if *(He/she)* survives me by 30 days. If *(He/she)* does not survive me by 30 days, I give the same sum of money to *(Name of alternate beneficiary)*, if *(He/she)* survives me by 30 days. If neither of the above persons survives me, this same sum of money should be disposed of with the residue of my estate.

Clause 7: Gifts under the Uniform Gifts or Transfers to Minors Act

All property given in this will to *(Name of minor child)* shall be given to *(Name of account custodian)*, as custodian for *(Name of minor child)* under the *(Specify Uniform Gifts or Transfers to Minors Act)* of *(Your state)*. If *(Name of custodian)* dies, resigns or is otherwise unable to serve as custodian, I appoint *(Name of successor custodian)* as successor custodian.

You need a clause like this for each custodial account you set up, and each minor child needs his or her own custodial account.

Clause 8: Residuary Estate

I give the rest of my estate, all the property I own that is not legally disposed of by this will or in any other manner, to my partner if *(He/she)* survives me by 30 days. In the event *(He/she)* does not survive me by 30 days, I leave the rest of my estate to my children, to be divided equally among them.

Clause 9: Signature

I subscribe my name to this will on the *(Date)* day of *(Month)*, 19 *(Year)*, at *(City, county and state)*, and declare that I am a legal and competent adult and that I did not enter into or sign this will under duress, constraint or undue influence.

(Your legal signature)

Clause 10: Attestation

On this *(Date)* day of *(Month)*, 19 *(Year)*, *(Your name)* declared to us, the undersigned, that this document was *(His/her)* will and asked us to serve as witnesses, signing our names accordingly. At the request of *(Your name)*, and in *(His/her)* presence, and in the presence of each other, all being present at the same time, we have signed our names as witnesses. We declare this to be the will of *(Your name)*, and that to the best of our knowledge, *(Your name)* is a competent adult and was under no undue influence, duress or constraint at the time of this signing. Under penalty of perjury, we declare that the foregoing is true and correct.

(Witness's signature)
(Witness's address)

(Witness's signature)
(Witness's address)

(Witness's signature)
(Witness's address)

Sample Will for an Unmarried Person with No Children Who Lives with a Partner

It is particularly important for unmarried people living together in committed relationships—lesbian and gay couples especially—to have wills designed to ensure that a partner gets the property the other wants him or her to have. Without a will, the property would go to the heirs according to the laws of the state and the partner would get nothing.

Last Will and Testament
of
(Your name)

Clause 1

I, *(Your name)*, a resident in *(Your city and state of residence)*, being of sound mind and not acting under any duress, fraud or undue influence of any person, declare this instrument as my LAST WILL AND TESTAMENT.

Clause 2: Revocation

I hereby revoke all prior wills and codicils by me.

Clause 3: Identification of Family

I am presently unmarried and have no living children.

The name of my partner is *(Name of partner)*, and all references in this will to my partner are to *(Him/her)*.

Clause 4: Appointment of Executor

I appoint *(Name of executor)* as executor of this will. If *(He/she)* cannot or will not serve in this capacity, I appoint *(Name of substitute executor)* as my substitute executor. In addition to all of the powers allowable under the laws of this state, I authorize and empower my executor to *(Itemize all of the additional powers and responsibilities you give your executor.)*.

I request that my executor be allowed to act without having to post any bond or other kind of security.

Clause 5: Disposition of Property

I leave all of my estate to *(Name of partner)*, if *(He/she)* survives me by 30 days. If *(He/she)* does not survive me by 30 days, my property should be distributed as follows:

I give *(Name of beneficiary)* my *(Description of property)*, if *(He/she)* survives me by 30 days. If *(He/she)* does not survive me by 30 days, I give the above-described property to *(Name of alternate beneficiary)*, if *(He/she)* survives me. If neither of the above persons survives me, the above-described property should be disposed of with the residue of my estate.

Repeat the above clause if necessary.

I give the sum of $*(Dollar amount)* to *(Name of beneficiary)*, if *(He/she)* survives me by 30 days. If *(He/she)* does not survive me by 30 days, I give the same sum of money to *(Name of alternate beneficiary)*, if *(He/she)* survives me. If neither of the above persons survives me by 30 days, the aforementioned sum should be disposed of with the residue of my estate.

Clause 6: Residuary Estate

I give the rest of my estate, all the property I own that is not legally disposed of by this will or in any other manner, to *(Name of partner)*. In the event *(He/she)* does not survive me, I give my residuary estate to *(Name of charity)*, located at *(Address of charity)*.

Clause 7: Signature

I subscribe my name to this will on the *(Date)* day of *(Month)*, 19 *(Year)*, at *(City, county and state)*, and declare that I am a legal and competent adult and that I did not enter into or sign this will under duress, constraint or undue influence.

   (Your legal signature)

Clause 8: Attestation

On this *(Date)* day of *(Month)*, 19 *(Year)*, *(Your name)* declared to us, the undersigned, that this document was *(His/her)* will and asked us to serve as witnesses, signing our names accordingly. At the request of *(Your name)*, and in *(His/her)* presence, and in the presence of each other, all being present at the same time, we have signed our names as witnesses. We declare this to be the will of *(Your name)*, and that to the best of our knowledge, *(Your name)* is a competent adult and was under no undue influence, duress or constraint at the time of this signing. Under penalty of perjury, we declare that the foregoing is true and correct.

(Witness's signature)
(Witness's address)

(Witness's signature)
(Witness's address)

(Witness's signature)
(Witness's address)

Special Clauses

Depending on your estate planning goals and needs, any number of special clauses might be appropriate for your will. Some of the most likely include the ones listed below.

Disinheritance Clause

In your will, you should provide for each of your living children as well as for the children of any of your children who are deceased. It can be just a token gift of a few dollars or a small item of personal property. If you don't remember each of these individuals in your will, you should specifically disinherit whomever you don't include. To not do so is to open yourself to the possibility that one of your heirs will contest your will, claiming you left him or her out by mistake. When this happens, your state may decide to give that person a share of your estate because by the laws of intestacy, he or she would be in line to inherit from you.

The following is an example of a clause you can use to disinherit someone:

In this will, I intentionally do not give anything to *(Name of person you disinherit)*, who is my *(Specify child or grandchild)*.

You'll notice when you read the celebrity wills in Appendix A that many celebrities are concerned about heirs who might make claims against their estates. This is especially true for those leading men who had relationships with many women.

Exoneration Clause

You can give real property such as a home or land to a beneficiary free of all encumbrances, or you can convey it with the debt attached. If you do the latter, your beneficiary must pay off the debt. Depending on the financial situation of your beneficiary and your own financial resources, you may want your gift of real property to come free of all its associated debt. If so, the following clause might be appropriate:

I give *(Description of real property)*, free and clear of all debt, including mortgages, trust deeds, liens and any other encumbrances, to *(Name of beneficiary)*, if *(He/she)* survives me by 30 days. I direct my executor to pay off, discharge and remove with funds from my residuary estate any and all indebtedness secured by mortgages, trust deeds, liens or other encumbrances existing against the aforementioned property at the time of my death and to obtain the release and discharge of all such encumbrances.

Payment of Death and Taxes Clause

It is always best to specify exactly how you want any debts and taxes your estate owes to be paid after you die, especially if you want certain assets to be sold in order to do that. Often, individuals specify that they want their debts and taxes to be paid by the residue of their estates, as the following clause indicates:

I direct my executor to pay all my debts and all inheritance, estate or other death taxes out of the residue of my estate.

Proportional Abatement Clause

Sometimes not enough funds remain in an estate to allow the executor to give to all of the beneficiaries the full amounts dictated by the will. This shortfall can be due to poor planning on the part of the willmaker; unanticipated claims against the estate; or failure to amend a will to account for changes in the willmaker's financial situation. To plan for this possibility, you can include a clause in your will that specifies how your estate should be divided if insufficient funds remain. The clause below allows you, in the event of a shortfall, to remember all of your beneficiaries, but it arranges to leave each beneficiary a smaller share on a proportional basis than he or she would have received had there been enough money:

Should the net assets of my estate be insufficient to satisfy in full all of the general and specific gifts I have made in this will, I direct that all gifts abate proportionally.

Business-Related Clause

As this book has indicated, business owners and those who own shares of businesses face special estate planning issues regarding the future of their businesses or business shares. Although you may be able to find better estate planning tools than a will to transfer ownership of a business or a business interest, using your will is certainly an option. Following are three clauses that can help a willmaker transfer business ownership. One is for a sole proprietorship, the next is for a partnership and the third is for shares of a corporation.

For a Sole Proprietorship:

I give to _(Name of beneficiary)_, if _(He/she)_ survives me by 30 days, my entire interest in _(Name of business)_, a sole proprietorship owned by me, with offices in _(Cities, counties and states)_. This gift includes all cash, bank accounts, inventory, equipment, machinery and other property used in connection with the business, upon condition that _(Name of beneficiary)_ pays or assumes responsibility for any business-related indebtedness I owe at the time of my death. If _(Name of beneficiary)_ does not survive me by 30 days or is unwilling to assume all the aforementioned debt, I direct that the aforementioned business be sold and the proceeds disposed of with the residue of my estate.

For a Partnership:

I give to _(Name of beneficiary)_, if _(He/she)_ survives me by 30 days, my entire interest in _(Name of business)_, a general partnership of which I am a general partner. This gift includes all my rights to specific partnership property, my rights to a proportionate share of the profits of the partnership, my rights to the return of my capital contributions to the partnership, my rights as a creditor of the partnership and any other rights that I have under a partnership agreement or otherwise as a withdrawing or deceased general partner of the partnership.

If _(Name of beneficiary)_ does not survive me by 30 days, I direct that the aforementioned interest in the aforementioned partnership be liquidated and the proceeds disposed of with the residue of my estate.

For Shares of a Corporation:

I give _(Number)_ shares of the common stock of _(Name of corporation)_ to _(Name of beneficiary)_, if _(He/she)_ survives me by 30 days. If _(He/she)_ does not survive me by 30 days, I give the aforementioned shares to *(Name of alternate beneficiary)*. If neither survives me by 30 days, I direct that the aforementioned shares be disposed of with the residue of my estate.

If the capital structure of *(Name of corporation)* is changed after the signing of this will, I give to *(Name of beneficiary)* the shares acquired by me by reason of ownership of the stock of said corporation through stock splits, stock dividends or the exercise of rights issued to me in exchange therefore, as in the sole judgment of my executor shall be the substantial equivalent at the time of my death of my ownership of the aforementioned number of shares of the present common stock of the aforementioned corporation.

Self-Proving Affidavit

After you die, the court may send the people who witnessed the signing of your will a copy of the will, along with an affidavit for them to sign and return to the court. In signing it, they verify that the signatures are yours and theirs and that all the appropriate legal procedures were followed. Depending on the circumstances after you die, your witnesses may have to appear in court to do this.

The problem with either process is that sometimes witnesses are difficult to locate or are deceased by the time a will is presented to the court. This delays the probate process.

To address this problem and to streamline the process, most states now allow use of a self-proving affidavit. The affidavit can be completed and signed at the same time you and your witnesses sign your will. A notary public fills out the self-proving affidavit and notarizes it after you and your witnesses sign it.

Figure 7.1 shows an example of a self-proving affidavit.

Giving Love and Saying Goodbye

Most people use their wills solely to dispose of their worldly possessions, everything they have accumulated over the years of their lives. Therefore, we often must read betwen the lines to gain a sense of their feelings for the individuals or organizations in their lives.

Henry Fonda, for example, started college with the ambition to become a newspaper reporter. But after two years, he went to work

FIGURE 7.1

✏ Self-Proving Affidavit

The State of _____
The County of _____

We, *(Your name)*, *(Name of witness)* and *(Name of witness)*, the testator and witnesses, respectively, whose names are signed to the attached or foregoing instrument, being first duly sworn, do hereby declare to the undersigned authority that the testator signed and executed the instrument as his or her last will and that he or she signed willingly or directed another to sign for him or her and he or she executed it as his or her free and voluntary act for the purposes therein expressed; and that each of the witnesses, in the presence and hearing of the testator, signed the will as witnesses and that to the best of his or her knowledge, the testator was at that time 18 or more years of age, of sound mind and under no constraint or undue influence.

(Your signature)
(Witness's signature)
(Witness's signature)

Subscribed, sworn and acknowledged before me by *(Your name)*, the testator, subscribed and sworn before me by *(Name of witness)* and *(Name of witness)*, witnesses, this *(Date)* day of *(Month)* 19 *(Year)*.

*(Official seal of
notary public)*

(Signature of notary)

Source: Adapted from *All-States Wills and Estate Planning Guide,* 1993 edition. The Judge Advocate General's School, U.S. Army, JA 262, *Legal Assistance Wills Guide,* pages 3-16–3-17 (May 1993). Reprinted by permission of the American Bar Association, Chicago, Illinois.

full-time at the Omaha Community Playhouse in Nebraska. In this cruci- ble of the theater, he began a career that ended with fame and glory. He must have had strong feelings about this regional theater, because he left the Omaha Community Playhouse his residuary estate. But he never described these feelings in his will.

My philosophy about writing a will is that we shouldn't limit our- selves to giving away our wealth when we have a chance to give much more. I believe we can use our wills to say what is in our hearts. No standard fill-in-the-blanks clause can express your feelings for you—you must let your heart be your guide. But for those who need a jump start to get their creative juices going, I will provide some examples.

To a Surviving Spouse:

To my wife, _____, I give all the love remaining in my heart. The love I have for you in my soul will travel with me to after-life's next journey. Be assured, my sweet wife, my love for you will extend into eternity. You saw me in failure and success, you saw me at my best and worst, and you saw me unlovable yet you loved me. I leave you with gratitude that I shared my life with you.

To a Surviving Child:

To my son, _____, I give my full respect and love. I watched you grow and experience more suffering at such an early age than most people experience in a lifetime. I was always so proud of how you bore all the bad times with such mature dignity and strength. I thought of you as a man in a boy's body. I can leave knowing you have everything you need inside you to make a good life for yourself.

To a Surviving Sister:

To my sister, _____, I give you all my love. Ever since the first day I saw you as a tiny baby, you have been the perfect little sister. I take with me many wonderful thoughts of our times together when we were growing up and of the special times we've shared as adults. I couldn't ask for more in a sister than what you have been to me.

Including such clauses in your will is not required, but doing so gives you an opportunity to express important feelings such as respect, love, gratitude, understanding, kindness and compassion. If you have always felt these sentiments in your heart but have never been able to express them, your will gives you the chance.

CHAPTER
EIGHT

Changing or Revoking Your Will or Trust

Chapter 1 described estate planning as a dynamic activity. That is, once you write your will, do not store it and never look at it again. If you fail to review your will and your life changes in important ways, the document won't reflect those changes and, therefore, may not accomplish what you would like it to. This chapter will provide a brief overview of when to change or cancel your will and how to do it.

Of all the wills in Appendix A, Clark Gable's is the saddest perhaps. He died of a heart attack before changing his will to provide for the child his wife was carrying at the time of his death. Like all of us, Gable was busy. At the time of his death, he was shooting *The Misfits* with Marilyn Monroe.

Reviewing Your Will for Changes

It's important to keep your will as up to date as possible so it reflects the current circumstances in your life and so you are assured that any assets you've acquired recently are addressed by either your will or some other estate planning tool. In fact, it's a good idea to review your will every one to two years. Even if things haven't changed in your life, you may still want to amend the document.

HOT TIP

If you wrote your will before 1981, you need to know that several major tax revisions have occurred since then. Therefore, review your will in light of those changes.

Life events that may require you to change your will include the following:

- You have a new child.
- One of your beneficiaries dies.
- Your marital status changes.
- Important assets or debts increase or decrease significantly.
- You begin or buy a business, end or sell a business or become part-owner of a business.
- Your executor dies or becomes incapacitated.
- Your minor child's personal or property guardian dies, becomes incapacitated or is unable to serve for some other reason.
- Your relationship with one of your beneficiaries changes.

HOT TIP

Depending on your state, if you divorce, the provisions in your will that apply to your ex-spouse may be automatically canceled.

- You move to a new state. (If you move, you must be certain that your will is valid in your new state of residence.)
- A state or federal law that affects estate planning is changed or a new law is adopted.
- You win the lottery!

How To Revise Your Will

You can change your will any time you want and as many times as you want, as long as you are physically and mentally competent when you do so. If a change is relatively minor—for example, you do not change your entire gift-giving scheme or add a testamentary trust to your will—you can change your will by preparing a codicil. A *codicil* is simply a written statement of the change you make. To be considered a valid part of your will, the codicil must be dated, witnessed and notarized according to the laws of your state and it must be kept with your will. Figure 8.1 provides an example of a codicil.

The number of codicils you can make to your will is unlimited. However, the more you make, the greater the likelihood that the codicils will create inconsistencies, contradictions or ambiguities in your will when they are read together. Therefore, it's best to limit codicils to two per will. If you want to make more than two changes to your will, revoke your current will and prepare a new one.

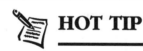 **HOT TIP**

Do not handwrite changes to your will. If you do, you may unwittingly invalidate it.

Revoking Your Will

If you prepare a new will, be sure to cancel or revoke your existing will by declaring in the new one that you revoke all previous wills. Even if your state allows you to revoke your will by destroying it—

FIGURE 8.1

✎ Sample Codicil

This is a sample codicil. It does not necessarily meet the codicil requirements of your state. It's provided as an example only.

First Codicil to the
Last Will and Testament
of
Your name

I, *(Your name)*, of *(City, county and state)*, hereby make, publish and declare this to be the First Codicil to the Last Will and Testament executed by me on the *(Date)* day of *Month*, 19 *(Year)*.

1. Additions to Will

I hereby add the following paragraph to clause *(Number of clause)* of my will: *(State exactly what you're adding)*

Repeat the above if necessary.

2. Revisions to Will

I hereby delete *(State exactly what you're deleting)* from clause *(Number of clause)* of my will and replace it with the following: *(State exactly what you're adding)*

Repeat the above if necessary.

3. Revocations to Will

I hereby revoke *(State exactly what you're deleting)* from clause *(Number of clause)* of my will.

Repeat the above if necessary.

4. Republication

I hereby remake and republish the unamended portions of my will.

In witness whereof, I hereby sign my name to this codicil on the *(Date)* day of *(Month)*, 19 *(Year)*, at *(City, county and state)*.

_____ *(Your signature)* _____

FIGURE 8.1 (continued)

✎ Sample Codicil

The foregoing instrument, consisting of *(Number)* pages, of which this is the last, was on the *(Date)* day of *(Month)*, 19 *(Year)*, signed and published by *(Your name)*, the testator, and declared by the testator to be the first codicil to *(His/her)* last will in the presence of each of us, who at the request of *(Your name)* and in *(His/her)* presence and in the presence of each other, now subscribe our names as witnesses.

(Signature of witness)   *(Signature of witness)*
(Name and address of witness)   *(Name and address of witness)*

The State of_____
The County of_____

We, *(Your name)*, *(Name of witness)* and *(Name of witness)*, the testator and the witnesses, respectively, whose names are signed to the attached or foregoing instrument, being first duly sworn, do hereby declare to the undersigned authority that the testator signed and executed the instrument as the first codicil to his or her last will and that he or she signed willingly and that he or she executed it as his or her free and voluntary act for the purposes therein expressed; and that each of the witnesses, in the presence and hearing of the testator, signed the codicil as witnesses and that to the best of his or her knowledge, the testator was at that time 18 or more years of age, of sound mind and under no constraint or undue influence.

(Your signature)
(Signature of witness)
(Signature of witness)

Subscribed, sworn and acknowledged before me by *(Your name)*, the testator, and subscribed and sworn before me by *(Name of witness)* and *(Name of witness)*, witnesses, this *(Date)* day of *(Month)*, 19 *(Year)*.

(Official seal of notary public)   *(Signature of notary)*

burning or defacing it, for example—it's always best to revoke a will in writing.

 **HOT TIP**

Don't use a pencil to write "revoked" or "canceled" on an out-of-date will. If you do, questions about the validity of your new will may be raised after your death. You can, however, use a pen.

Changing or Revoking a Trust

The only kind of trust you can change is a revocable living trust. Possible modifications to a trust include changing the beneficiaries or the trustee and amending the instructions or terms of the trust.

To modify a trust, you must prepare and date an amendment. This is a fairly straightforward process. Do not simply alter the original agreement because the validity of the change could be questioned later.

 **HOT TIP**

You won't need an amendment to add or remove assets from a trust because doing so is an automatic benefit of a revocable living trust.

To revoke a trust, you probably must do so with a signed and dated document that formally cancels it. Both modifications and revocations should be done with the help of an attorney.

Planning for the Possibility of Mental or Physical Incapacitation

Planning for the possibility that someday you may become temporarily or permanently incapacitated and unable to make your own decisions about your health and medical care should be an essential part of estate planning. It is especially important given that today's sophisticated technology allows lives to be continued almost indefinitely.

If you become incapacitated, decisions may have to be made regarding your personal financial and legal affairs and if you're a business owner, your business affairs also must be tended to. Planning for how someone else will handle these matters if you're not able to is another aspect of estate planning.

This chapter will review some of the tools you can use to control your health and medical care should you become unable to speak for yourself. For example, you can give someone a durable power of attorney for health care and prepare a living will. It will also briefly discuss tools you can use to ensure that your personal and business affairs— both financial and legal—are well managed.

Why Health Care Planning Is Important

Anyone who has been in the hospital or has had a relative or close friend hospitalized is aware just how quickly medical bills can mount. Even if you have good health insurance, a serious illness or accident can quickly use up any savings you have and maybe even force you to liquidate valuable assets, diminishing the size of your estate. This is a very real possibility if you are critically ill or injured and life-sustaining measures are used to keep you alive as long as possible.

An increasing number of people want to exercise control over the health care they receive when they are terminally ill or critically injured and are unable to speak for themselves. They may want this control for any number of reasons, including the following:

- They don't want to be kept alive at all costs.
- They don't want their families to watch them die little by little or to second-guess what they would want if they could speak.
- They want to spare their families from having to petition the court to have conservators appointed to handle their affairs for them.
- They don't want to see the estates they worked hard to build depleted by costly medical care.

Therefore, many people prepare health care directives—living wills and durable powers of attorney for health care.

The federal government has encouraged the use of health care directives. In 1990, Congress passed the Patient Self-Determination Act. This law says that any facility receiving Medicaid or Medicare monies must provide patients with written information about health care directives at the time of their admission. It also says that if a patient chooses to prepare a health care directive, the facility must place this directive with his or her medical records. Many facilities also provide patients with standard forms they can use to prepare their own living wills or durable powers of attorney for health care.

What Is a Living Will?

A *living will* is a written document that speaks for you if you are too ill to speak for yourself. It states your wishes regarding the use of machines and treatments designed to sustain your life. These machines and treatments include respirators, breathing tubes, cardiac assist pumps, intravenous tubes, artificial nutrition tubes, artificial hydration, dialysis and cardiopulmonary resuscitation. You can use a living will to provide your doctors with "do not resuscitate" instructions, "do all you can" instructions or something in between.

When you write a living will, you usually specify the medical and health care you *don't* want when you're dying, but you can also specify what you *do* want.

Preparing a Living Will

You can write your own living will or health care directive without the help of an attorney by using a fill-in-the-blanks living will form available from a hospital in your area, your local bar association or an area agency on aging. You can also obtain a free living will form that is legal in your particular state by contacting the national nonprofit organization Choice in Dying (200 Varick Street, New York, NY 10012-4810; 800-989-WILL). You can find the organization's form for Texas residents in Appendix C.

 **HOT TIP**

Because laws relating to living wills change rapidly, if you use a fill-in-the-blanks living will, make sure it reflects the most current laws in your state.

Using a standard form is fine as long as it adheres to the laws of your state; however, like a fill-in-the-blanks will, it may not address all of your concerns or adequately reflect your preferences in regard to specific treatments. Therefore, you may prefer a living will that is customized to reflect your particular needs and concerns (see Figure 9.1 for suggestions). You can prepare it yourself, using the standard form for your state as a starting point, or you can get the help of an attorney.

 **HOT TIP**

If you are a resident of more than one state, or if you take an annual vacation in another state, prepare living wills for both states. You should also execute legal durable health care powers of attorney for both states.

Store your living will in a fireproof safe at home or in a safe-deposit box. Make sure someone besides you knows the combination to the safe or has a key to the safe-deposit box. Also, give a copy of your living will to your spouse, your unmarried partner, a close family member or a good friend. Review the document with that person so that if it must be activated, he or she will feel comfortable doing so.

Most states require that people with living wills let their doctors know they've written them. Even if your state does not require this, it's still an excellent idea to do so. Better yet, review your living will with your doctor so you can be assured that he or she feels comfortable with its directives. If your doctor is not comfortable with the document and would be reluctant to enforce it, you can switch to a more sympathetic physician. Ask your doctor to keep a copy of the living will with your medical records.

Legal Requirements for Living Wills

All states recognize living wills. However, every state has its own criteria for what makes a living will legally valid and enforceable.

FIGURE 9.1

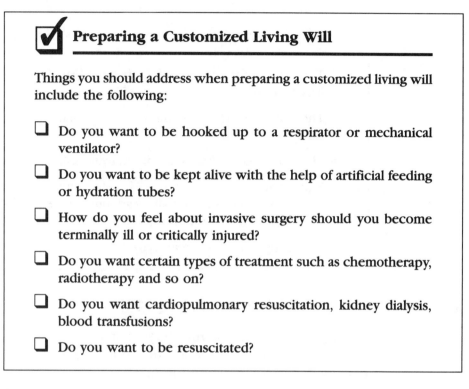

☑ **Preparing a Customized Living Will**

Things you should address when preparing a customized living will include the following:

❑ Do you want to be hooked up to a respirator or mechanical ventilator?

❑ Do you want to be kept alive with the help of artificial feeding or hydration tubes?

❑ How do you feel about invasive surgery should you become terminally ill or critically injured?

❑ Do you want certain types of treatment such as chemotherapy, radiotherapy and so on?

❑ Do you want cardiopulmonary resuscitation, kidney dialysis, blood transfusions?

❑ Do you want to be resuscitated?

Generally, however, most legally valid living wills have certain characteristics. They include those listed in Figure 9.2.

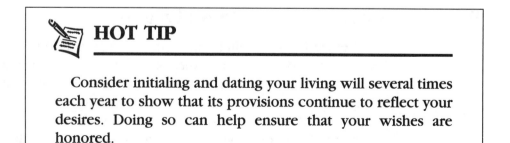

🗒 **HOT TIP**

Consider initialing and dating your living will several times each year to show that its provisions continue to reflect your desires. Doing so can help ensure that your wishes are honored.

FIGURE 9.2

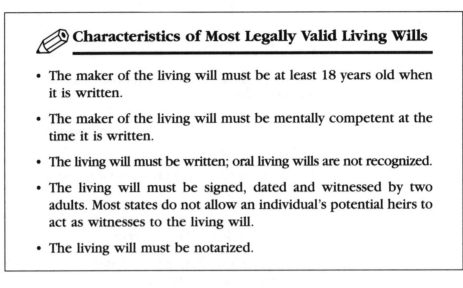

> ✏️ **Characteristics of Most Legally Valid Living Wills**
>
> - The maker of the living will must be at least 18 years old when it is written.
>
> - The maker of the living will must be mentally competent at the time it is written.
>
> - The living will must be written; oral living wills are not recognized.
>
> - The living will must be signed, dated and witnessed by two adults. Most states do not allow an individual's potential heirs to act as witnesses to the living will.
>
> - The living will must be notarized.

Changing or Revoking a Living Will

You can change or revoke your living will whenever you want. However, before doing either, find out your state's requirements for making a change or revocation legal.

All you probably need to do to revoke your living will is write on it that it's no longer valid. It's a good idea to get back any copies you have given to people and do the same with those copies. If you've registered your living will with a government agency, as is required in some states, be sure to get it back, too.

When Will a Living Will Be Activated?

Generally, your living will cannot be activated until you are near death and two doctors, sometimes one, have stated in writing that you're unable to make your own decisions and are terminally ill or permanently unconscious. This means that even if you are in a great deal of pain but death is not imminent, your living will won't go into effect.

Normally, if your doctors are aware that you have a living will, and if the document is legally valid, they are expected to comply with it. However, sometimes doctors ignore the directives of a living will or drag their feet when processing the paperwork required to activate it. They may do this for several reasons:

- The doctors are uncomfortable with the living will's provisions.
- The patient's family does not want the living will to be activated and puts pressure on the doctors not to follow the patient's wishes.
- The doctors do not agree on the definition of "terminally ill" or "permanently unconscious," or their opinions differ regarding the patient's prognosis.
- The living will's provisions are too vague to enforce.

To prevent your family from interfering with the activation of your living will, talk with them after you write it, explain what your desires are and why, and answer any questions they have. If you do this, they may be more apt to understand and respect your wishes.

If you are terminally ill or critically injured and your doctor will not comply with the directives in your living will, your family can ask that you be transferred to a more sympathetic physician. However, switching at that point can be difficult. Therefore, your family may need to consult with an attorney who specializes in elder care law. Sometimes such cases must be decided by a court.

 **HOT TIP**

All states exempt doctors from prosecution if their compliance with a patient's health care directive causes the patient to die. In fact, some states prosecute doctors who fail to comply with the patient's wishes.

Enforcing Your Living Will with a Durable Power of Attorney for Health Care

Giving someone a durable power of attorney for heath care is one of the best things you can do to help ensure that your living will is enforced when the time comes. The person to whom you give a durable power of attorney for health care can advocate for you, speak on your behalf and actively push for activation of your living will if your doctor or family is reluctant. That person can also make medical and health decisions on your behalf when you are dying. In some states, this person can also make such decisions when you are physically or mentally incapacitated but death is not an immediate threat. Therefore, a durable power of attorney for health care is a more comprehensive and powerful legal tool than a living will. Appendix D includes a sample durable power of attorney for health care valid in Texas.

HOT TIP

It's a good idea to prepare a living will and a durable power of attorney for health care at the same time.

The person to whom you give this power must be at least 18 years old and should be someone you trust implicitly and whom you feel has the personal strength to make potentially difficult decisions for you. Also, be sure this person is willing to accept the important responsibility you want to entrust to him or her. In addition, check with your state to find out whether it has any restrictions regarding whom you can appoint. For example, you may not be allowed to appoint your doctor or your residential care provider.

HOT TIP

Instruct the person to whom you give power of attorney that if you are put in a nursing home or an assisted-living facility and are later transferred to a hospital, that person should make sure that your living will is transferred with you; should make sure that your doctor is aware of your living will; and should make sure that these documents are filed with your hospital medical records.

The best kind of durable power of attorney for health care is one that not only specifies the kinds of medical treatment you do and don't want but also spells out your values and personal beliefs in regard to life-sustaining measures, pain, the relative cost of various procedures and treatments and other quality-of-life issues. You may also want to describe what you consider to be an acceptable quality of life. In your instructions to the person you give power of attorney, be as clear and specific as possible so that nothing is left to interpretation. And don't merely write this information down; talk about it in person with the individual you want to act as your agent.

 **HOT TIP**

Think carefully before giving your spouse a health care durable power of attorney because it may be difficult for him or her to act dispassionately when the time comes. Also, if your living will dictates an end to life-sustaining treatments and your spouse objects, it's unlikely that your doctors will activate your living will.

As with a living will, you can use a fill-in-the-blanks form to create a durable power of attorney for health care, as long as it meets the requirements of your state. The same kinds of organizations that can provide you with a standard form for a living will can give you a standard form for a durable power of attorney for health care. You can also hire an attorney to write one that reflects your particular needs and concerns.

 **HOT TIP**

The more specific your durable power of attorney is, the more likely it is to be honored.

Just as you should do with your will and living will, it's a good idea to periodically review your durable power of attorney for health care to ensure that it still reflects your wishes. Some states require this.

Changing or Revoking a Durable Power of Attorney for Health Care

You can change or revoke a durable power of attorney for health care whenever you wish, as long as you are mentally competent. If you change it, make sure you adhere to the laws of your state. If you revoke it, prepare a formal notice of revocation.

If you gave copies of the document creating the power of attorney to others, get them back and throw them away.

Figure 9.3 outlines the basic steps in preparing a health care directive.

If You Don't Have a Living Will

If you become critically ill and you don't have a living will, the doctor in charge of your care will decide what treatment you receive. Generally, the doctor will take a conservative approach to your medical care and will do whatever is necessary to sustain your life. This approach to your care is, in part, a logical outcome of the doctor's education, the focus of which is saving lives. It is also a function of the medical profession's code of ethics, not to mention a response to the doctor's fear of being sued by a patient's family.

Although your doctor may consult with your spouse and other close family members about what to do when you are dying, the doctor is not obligated to comply with your family's wishes.

If your family wants to stop certain kinds of medical care and treatment because they believe you wouldn't want it, and if your doctor is not willing to comply, a formal hearing may be held to resolve the stale-

 **HOT TIP**

Some states allow a family member, often a spouse, to make the decision regarding the use or continued use of life-sustaining measures, going under the assumption that this person knows what you would want.

FIGURE 9.3

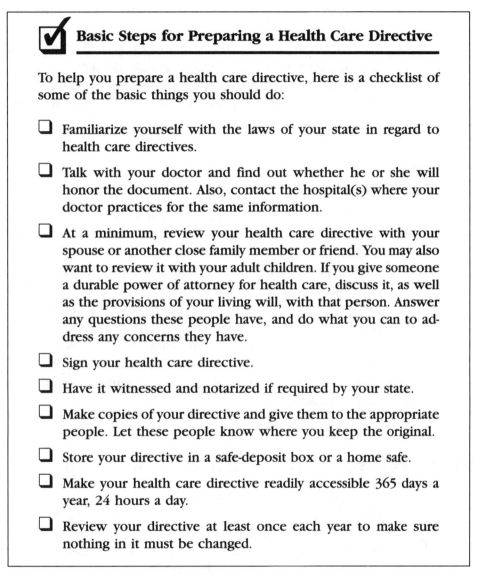

✓ Basic Steps for Preparing a Health Care Directive

To help you prepare a health care directive, here is a checklist of some of the basic things you should do:

❑ Familiarize yourself with the laws of your state in regard to health care directives.

❑ Talk with your doctor and find out whether he or she will honor the document. Also, contact the hospital(s) where your doctor practices for the same information.

❑ At a minimum, review your health care directive with your spouse or another close family member or friend. You may also want to review it with your adult children. If you give someone a durable power of attorney for health care, discuss it, as well as the provisions of your living will, with that person. Answer any questions these people have, and do what you can to address any concerns they have.

❑ Sign your health care directive.

❑ Have it witnessed and notarized if required by your state.

❑ Make copies of your directive and give them to the appropriate people. Let these people know where you keep the original.

❑ Store your directive in a safe-deposit box or a home safe.

❑ Make your health care directive readily accessible 365 days a year, 24 hours a day.

❑ Review your directive at least once each year to make sure nothing in it must be changed.

mate. This hearing can cost your family money and also may be emotionally draining for them. Another option is to find a new doctor more sympathetic to their wishes. This may also require the involvement of the court. A third option is for your family to petition the court to have a conservator appointed who will make medical decisions for you.

If you are in a committed but unmarried relationship, and especially if you are in a same-sex relationship, it is unlikely that your doctor will consult your partner about what to do. The best way to ensure that your partner is consulted by your doctor is to give that person a durable power of attorney for health care. Your partner should also have a copy of your living will.

Conservators

If your family must petition the court to appoint a conservator to make health care decisions for you, the process can be costly and emotionally difficult for your loved ones.

After the court is petitioned, a hearing will be held to establish your incompetence. If the court agrees that you are no longer in a condition to make good decisions for yourself, it will name someone to do it for you. Often that person is a family member.

A key disadvantage of involving the court is that frequently it must okay the transactions your court-appointed representative wants to make on your behalf. This can involve paperwork and red tape and may slow things down.

Burial or Cremation Instructions and Organ Donation

You can make things easier for your loved ones immediately after your death if you write down your desires regarding your funeral arrangements. Even better, make the arrangements before you die, and write down the details of what you've arranged. Indicate in your written instructions whether you want to be buried or cremated and whether you want your organs donated. Describe your funeral or memorial service—who will speak, where it should be held, music to be played and so on. If you have purchased a burial plot and arranged for a casket, write down these details, too. Be sure that your executor and your spouse or unmarried partner know where you store the instructions.

HOT TIP

Neither your family nor your executor is legally bound to follow your burial instructions. However, if you write them down and discuss your desires with these people, you increase the chance that they will follow your wishes.

The Uniform Anatomical Gift Act allows people to indicate whether they want certain organs to be donated to others after their death. Donating an organ so someone else may live is perhaps the greatest gift you can give to anyone after you die.

As a part of planning for your death, it is a good idea to obtain an organ donor card from your state's department of motor vehicles. Complete the card, and have it witnessed. Depending on your state's requirements, you may attach the completed organ donor card to your driver's license. You can also obtain an organ donor card by contacting the Living Bank (P.O. Box 6725, Houston, TX 77265; 713-528-2971).

HOT TIP

You can state your wishes regarding organ donation in the paperwork creating a durable power of attorney for health care.

Be sure that your doctor, close family members and the person to whom you give a durable power of attorney for health care are aware of your desires regarding organ donation.

Durable Power of Attorney

In addition to giving someone the power to make health and medical care decisions for you and the power to get your living will enforced, you may also want to give someone a *durable power of attorney.* This power of attorney differs from a health care power of attorney in that it deals with financial and business transactions. Therefore, the person to whom you give a durable health care power of attorney may not be the person to whom you give a durable power of attorney because the jobs require different skills.

You can give someone a durable power of attorney that applies to your general personal or business affairs. It can also be set up to apply to a specific transaction. Regardless of what kind of power of attorney you give someone, you must do it while you are mentally competent and understand your actions.

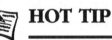 **HOT TIP**

Before you give someone a power of attorney for your personal or business affairs, check with your bank to make sure that the document allows immediate access to your funds in the bank. If not, find out what other documentation is necessary, and prepare it, too. In addition, it's a good idea to get the bank's written approval of your power of attorney after you've prepared it.

For people with modest estates who are concerned about how their personal or business affairs would be managed if they became incapacitated, a durable power of attorney can be an inexpensive alternative to establishing a trust and naming a trustee to manage a person's

---

 **HOT TIP**

The person to whom you give power of attorney can make *inter vivos* gifts on your behalf if you specify so. However, be aware that if the person makes such gifts, he or she may suffer negative tax consequences. Check with an attorney!

---

affairs. In fact, a durable power of attorney is sometimes called a poor man's trust. You can find a sample durable power of attorney for health care form in Appendix D.

If you don't give someone durable power of attorney and you become unable to manage your own affairs, your family can ask the court to appoint a guardian for you. However, like the appointment process for a conservator, it can be expensive and emotionally difficult for your family. Furthermore, the process can take time, which means that until a guardian is appointed, your affairs will be in limbo. Also, the person appointed to manage your affairs may not be someone you would want making decisions for you if you could speak on your own behalf.

 HOT TIP

When you establish a durable power of attorney, you must explicitly state that it is durable.

Appendix A
Wills of
Famous People

SUPERIOR COURT OF WASHINGTON FOR KING COUNTY

In the Matter of the Estate)
of   )
)
)
KURT D. COBAIN,   )
)
)
              Deceased.   )
_____)

No. 94-4-02203-0

VERIFIED PETITION FOR LETTERS
OF ADMINISTRATION AND ORDER
GRANTING NONINTERVENTION POWERS

1. <u>Petitioner</u>. Petitioner COURTNEY LOVE-COBAIN is the surviving spouse of the Decedent and is not a creditor of the estate.

2. <u>Jurisdiction</u>. Decedent died on April 5, 1994, was a resident of King County, Washington, and left property in King County, Washington, subject to project. No Will has been found.

3. <u>Notice</u>. Notice is not necessary because Petitioner Courtney Love-Cobain is the surviving spouse of the Decedent and Decedent left no issue of a prior marriage.

4. <u>Solvency</u>. To Petitioner's knowledge, the assets of the estate exceed expenses, taxes, debts and claims of creditors, and the estate is solvent. The assets of the estate will exceed $1,200,000. All known expenses, debts, etc. are anticipated to be less than $740,000.

5. <u>Heirs</u>. The names, addresses, relationships and ages of the heirs who survived Decedent are reflected on Exhibit A attached hereto and incorporated herein by this reference.

6. <u>Nominees</u>. Courtney Love-Cobain, a qualified person, resides in Seattle, King County, Washington, and seeks her appointment as Administratrix/Personal Representative of Decedent's estate.

7. <u>Bond</u>. Petitioner requests that no bond be required herein because Petitioner is the Decedent's surviving spouse.

WHEREFORE, Petitioner prays for an Order as follows:

1. That Letters of Administration be issued to the Petitioner;

2. That no bond be required herein;

3. That the estate be declared solvent and that upon the filing of her oath herein, the Petitioner, as Administratrix/Personal Representative, be granted nonintervention powers; and

4. For such other and further relief as the Court deems just and proper under the circumstances.

DATED: ___May 13___ , 1994.

GORES & BLAIS

_____
Celeste Norris Mitchel, WSBA No. 11139
Attorneys for Petitioner

STATE OF __New York__)
) ss.
COUNTY OF __Rockland__)

The undersigned, being first duly sworn upon oath, deposes and says:

I am the Petitioner named in the foregoing Petition; that I have read the Petition, know the contents thereof and believe the same to be true.

_____
Courtney Love-Cobain, Petitioner

SUBSCRIBED AND SWORN to before me this __12th__ day of __May__ 1994.

(Seal or stamp)

_____
Printed name: _____
Notary Public in and for the
State of __New York__
My appointment expires __2/05/96__

EXHIBIT A

Name and Address	Relationship	Age
Courtney Love-Cobain	Surviving Spouse	L
Frances B. Cobain	Daughter	M

LAST WILL
OF
HENRY J. FONDA

I, HENRY J. FONDA, a resident of Los Angeles County, California, declare this to be my Last Will and revoke all former Wills and Codicils thereto.

FIRST: I declare that I am married to Shirlee Adams Fonda, and that we have no issue. I further declare that I have three children by previous marriages: My daughters Jane Fonda Hayden and Amy Fonda Fishman, and my son Peter Henry Fonda.

SECOND: It is my wish that there be no funeral or memorial service at the time of my death, and that my remains be promptly cremated and disposed of without ceremony of any kind.

THIRD: I am providing primarily for my wife Shirlee and my daughter Amy because they are dependent upon me for their support. I have made no provision in this Will for Jane or Peter, or for their families, solely because in my opinion they are financially independent, and my decision is not in any sense a measure of my deep affection for them.

FOURTH: I give to my wife Shirlee, if she is living 30 days after the date of my death, all of my personal effects, clothing and automobiles, together with any interest I may have in our furniture, furnishings and objects of art. Should Shirlee not be living 30 days after the date of my death then I give my personal effects and clothing to my son Peter to be disposed of as he deems best, and the balance of this gift shall lapse.

FIFTH: I give $200,000.00 to my daughter Amy, if she is living 90 days after the date of my death. If Amy is not living at that time then this gift shall lapse.

SIXTH: I give the residue of my estate, of whatsoever kind and nature, and wheresoever situated, to Shirlee Adams Fonda, if she is living 90 days after the date of my death.

SEVENTH: If Shirlee is not living 90 days after the date of my death, then I give the aforesaid residue of my estate to the Omaha Community Playhouse, at Omaha, Nebraska, to be used for such capital improvements, and for the maintenance and operation thereof, as the governing body of said Playhouse deems proper, this gift to be known as ''The Henry and Shirlee Fonda Bequest.''

EIGHTH: I direct that all Federal and state estate, inheritance and succession taxes payable by reason of my death, and whether or not attributable to properties subject to probate administration, be charged to and paid from the residue of my probate estate as a whole, without allocation to or apportionment among the residuary beneficiaries.

NINTH: Except as otherwise provided herein, I have intentionally and with full knowledge omitted to provide for my heirs, including any persons who may claim to be my issue. If any beneficiary under this Will, or any legal heir of mine, or any person claiming under any of them, shall contest this Will or attack or seek to impair or invalidate this Will, or any part or provision hereof, or conspire with or voluntarily assist anyone attempting to do any of those things, in that event I specifically disinherit each such person and all legacies, bequests, devises and interests given under this Will to that person shall lapse and be forfeited, and shall be disposed of as if such person (together with anyone claiming through such person under any anti-lapse law) had predeceased me without issue.

TENTH: I appoint Shirlee Adams Fonda, Peter Henry Fonda and Richard M. Rosenthal as Executors of this Will, and should any one or more thereof be dead or unable or unwilling so to act, or should any one or more of them fail to complete the administration of my estate, then I appoint the remaining persons or person as Executors or Executor.

No bond shall be required of any Executor acting hereunder, and the Executors or Executor acting hereunder shall have full power and authority to lease, sell, exchange or encumber the whole or any part of my estate, at public or private sale, with or without notice, subject only to such confirmation of court as may be required by law; shall have full power and authority to continue to operate any business or other enterprise in which my estate has an interest, the profits and losses therefrom to inure to and be chargeable against my estate as a whole; and shall have full power and authority to distribute the assets of my estate in cash or in kind, allocating assets among the beneficiaries and following such procedure as said Executor deems reasonable.

The Executors or Executor acting hereunder are further empowered to invest and reinvest surplus moneys of this estate in such types of investments, both real and personal, as may be selected in the discretion of such Executors or Executor including corporate obligations of every kind, preferred or common stocks and common trust funds, subject only to such authorization of court as may be required by law.

IN WITNESS WHEREOF, I have hereunto set my hand this __22__ day of __January__ , 1981.

Date __Sep 13, 1982__

Attest: Los Angeles County Clerk

By: _____ Deputy

Henry J. Fonda

On the date written below, HENRY J. FONDA declared to us, the undersigned, that this instrument, consisting of 3 pages including the page signed by us as witnesses, was his Will and requested us to act as witnesses to it. He thereupon signed this Will in our presence, all of us being present at the same time.

At this time HENRY J. FONDA is over eighteen years of age and appears to be of sound mind. We have no knowledge of any facts indicating that this instrument, or any part of it, was procured by duress, menace, fraud or undue influence. Each of us is now over eighteen years of age. We now, in his presence and in the presence of each other, subscribe our names as witnesses.

Executed on __January 22__ , 1981, at __Los Angeles__ , California.

We declare under penalty of perjury that the foregoing is true and correct.

_____ Residing at _____
_____
_____ Residing at _____
_____
_____ Residing at _____
_____

LAST WILL AND TESTAMENT OF ELVIS A. PRESLEY, DECEASED
FILED AUGUST 22, 1977
LAST WILL AND TESTAMENT
OF
ELVIS A. PRESLEY

I, ELVIS A. PRESLEY, a resident and citizen of Shelby
County, Tennessee, being of sound mind and disposing memory,
do hereby make, publish and declare this instrument to be my
last will and testament, hereby revoking any and all wills and
codicils by me at any time heretofore made.

ITEM I
Debts, Expenses and Taxes

I direct my Executor, hereinafter named, to pay all of
my matured debts and my funeral expenses, as well as the costs
and expenses of the administration of my estate, as soon after
my death as practicable. I further direct that all estate,
inheritance, transfer and succession taxes which are payable
by reason of my death, whether or not with respect to property
passing under this will, be paid out of my residuary estate;
and I hereby waive on behalf of my estate any right to recover
from any person any part of such taxes so paid. My Executor,
in his sole discretion, may pay from my domiciliary estate all
or any portion of the costs of ancillary administration and
similar proceedings in other jurisdictions.

ITEM II
Instructions Concerning Personal
Property: Enjoyment in Specie

I anticipate that included as a part of my property
and estate at the time of my death will be tangible personal
property of various kinds, characters and values, including
trophies and other items accumulated by me during my
professional career. I hereby specifically instruct all
concerned that my Executor, herein appointed, shall have
complete freedom and discretion as to disposal of any and all
such property so long as he shall act in good faith and in the
best interest of my estate and my beneficiaries, and his
discretion so exercised shall not be subject to question by
anyone whomsoever.

I hereby expressly authorize my Executor and my Trustee respectively and successively, to permit any beneficiary of any and all trusts created hereunder to enjoy in specie the use or benefit of any household goods, chattels, or other tangible personal property (exclusive of choses in action, cash, stocks, bonds or other securities) which either my Executor or my Trustee may receive in kind, and my Executor and my Trustee shall not be liable for any consumption, damage, injury to or loss of any tangible property so used, nor shall the beneficiaries of any trusts hereunder or their executors or administrators be liable for any consumption, damage, injury to or loss of any tangible personal property so used.

ITEM III
Real Estate

If I am the owner of any real estate at the time of my death, I instruct and empower my Executor and my Trustee (as the case may be) to hold such real estate for investment, or to sell same, or any portion thereof, as my Executor or my Trustee (as the case may be) shall in his sole judgment determine to be for the best interest of my estate and the beneficiaries thereof.

ITEM IV
Residuary Trust

After payment of all debts, expenses and taxes as directed under ITEM I hereof, I give, devise, and bequeath all the rest, residue, and remainder of my estate, including all lapsed legacies and devises, and any property over which I have a power of appointment, to my Trustee, hereinafter named, in trust for the following purposes:

(a) The Trustee is directed to take, hold, manage, invest and reinvest the corpus of the trust and to collect the income therefrom in accordance with the rights, powers, duties, authority and discretion hereinafter set forth. The Trustee is directed to pay all the expenses, taxes and costs incurred in the management of the trust estate out of the income thereof.

(b) After payment of all expenses, taxes and costs incurred in the management of the trust estate, the Trustee is authorized to accumulate the net income or to pay or apply so much of the net income and such portion of the principal at any time and from time to time for the health, education, support, comfortable maintenance and welfare of: (1) my daughter, Lisa Marie Presley, and any other lawful issue I might have, (2) my grandmother, Minnie Mae Presley, (3) my father, Vernon E. Presley, and (4) such other relatives of mine living at the time of my death who in the absolute discretion of my Trustee are in need of emergency assistance for any of the above mentioned purposes and the Trustee is able to make such distribution without affecting the ability of the trust to meet the present needs of the first three numbered categories of beneficiaries herein mentioned or to meet the reasonably expected future needs of the first three classes of beneficiaries herein mentioned. Any decision of the Trustee as to whether or not distribution shall be made, and also as to the amount of such distribution, to any of the persons described hereunder shall be final and conclusive and not subject to question by any legatee or beneficiary hereunder.

(c) Upon the death of my father, Vernon E. Presley, the Trustee is instructed to make no further distributions to the fourth category of beneficiaries and such beneficiaries shall cease to have any interest whatsoever in this trust.

(d) Upon the death of both my said father and my said grandmother, the Trustee is directed to divide the Residuary Trust into separate and equal trusts, creating one such equal trust for each of my lawful children then surviving and one such equal trust for the living issue collectively, if any, of any deceased child of mine. The share, if any, for the issue of any such deceased child, shall immediately vest in such issue in equal shares but shall be subject to the provisions of ITEM V herein. Separate books and records shall be kept for each trust, but it shall not be necessary that a physical division of the assets be made as to each trust.

The Trustee may from time to time distribute the whole or any part of the net income or principal from each of the aforesaid trusts as the Trustee, in its uncontrolled discretion, considers necessary or desirable to provide for the comfortable support, education, maintenance, benefit and general welfare of each of my children. Such distributions may be made directly to such beneficiary or to any person standing in the place of a parent or to the guardian of the person of such beneficiary and without responsibility on my Trustee to see to the application of any such distributions and in making such distributions, the Trustee shall take into account all other sources of funds known by the Trustee to be available for each respective beneficiary for such purpose.

(e) As each of my respective children attains the age of twenty-five (25) years and provided that both my father and grandmother then be deceased, the trust created hereunder for such child shall terminate, and all the remainder of the assets then contained in said trust shall be distributed to such child so attaining the age of twenty-five (25) years outright and free of further trust.

(f) If any of my children for whose benefit a trust has been created hereunder should die before attaining the age of twenty-five (25) years, then the trust created for such child shall terminate on his death, and all remaining assets then contained in said trust shall be distributed outright and free of further trust and in equal shares to the surviving issue of such deceased child but subject to the provisions of ITEM V herein; but if there be no such surviving issue, then to the brothers and sisters of such deceased child in equal shares, the issue of any other deceased child being entitled collectively to their deceased parent's share. Nevertheless, if any distribution otherwise becomes payable outright and free of trust under the provisions of this paragraph (f) of this ITEM IV of my will to a beneficiary for whom the Trustee is then administering a trust for the benefit of such beneficiary under the provisions of this last will and testament, such distribution shall not be paid outright to such beneficiary but shall be added to and become a part of the trust so being administered for such beneficiary by the Trustee.

ITEM V
Distribution to Minor Children

If any share of corpus of any trust established under this will becomes distributable outright and free of trust to any beneficiary before said beneficiary has attained the age of eighteen (18) years, then said share shall immediately vest in said beneficiary, but the Trustee shall retain possession of such share during the period in which such beneficiary is under the age of eighteen (18) years, and, in the meantime, shall use and expend so much of the income and principal of each share as the Trustee deems necessary and desirable for the care, support and education of such beneficiary, and any income not so expended shall be added to the principal. The Trustee shall have with respect to each share so retained all the power and discretion had with respect to such trust generally.

ITEM VI
Alternate Distributees

In the event that all of my descendants should be deceased at any time prior to the time for the termination of the trusts provided for herein, then in such event all of my estate and all the assets of every trust to be created hereunder (as the case may be) shall then be distributed outright in equal shares to my heirs at law per stirpes.

ITEM VII
Unenforceable Provisions

If any provisions of this will are unenforceable, the remaining provisions shall, nevertheless, be carried into effect.

ITEM VIII
Life Insurance

If my estate is the beneficiary of any life insurance on my life at the time of my death, I direct that the proceeds therefrom will be used by my Executor in payment of the debts, expenses and taxes listed in ITEM I of this will, to the extent deemed advisable by the Executor. All such proceeds not so used are to be used by my Executor for the purpose of satisfying the devises and bequests contained in ITEM IV herein.

ITEM IX
Spendthrift Provision

I direct that the interest of any beneficiary in principal or income of any trust created hereunder shall not be subject to claims of creditors or others, nor to legal process, and may not be voluntarily or involuntarily alienated or encumbered except as herein provided. Any bequests contained herein for any female shall be for her sole and separate use, free from the debts, contracts and control of any husband she may ever have.

ITEM X
Proceeds From Personal Services

All sums paid after my death (either to my estate or to any of the trusts created hereunder) and resulting from personal services rendered by me during my lifetime, including, but not limited to, royalties of all nature, concerts, motion picture contracts, and personal appearances shall be considered to be income, notwithstanding the provisions of estate and trust law to the contrary.

ITEM XI
Executor and Trustee

I appoint as Executor of this, my last will and testament, and as Trustee of every trust required to be created hereunder, my said father.

I hereby direct that my said father shall be entitled by his last will and testament, duly probated, to appoint a successor Executor of my estate, as well as a successor Trustee or successor Trustees of all the trusts to be created under my last will and testament.

If, for any reason, my said father be unable to serve or to continue to serve as Executor and/or as Trustee, or if he be deceased and shall not have appointed a successor Executor or Trustee, by virtue of his last will and testament as stated-above, then I appoint National Bank of Commerce, Memphis, Tennessee, or its successor or the institution with which it may merge, as successor Executor and/or as successor Trustee of all trusts required to be established hereunder.

None of the appointees named hereunder, including any appointment made by virtue of the last will and testament of my said father, shall be required to furnish any bond or security for performance of the respective fiduciary duties required hereunder, notwithstanding any rule of law to the contrary.

ITEM XII
Powers, Duties, Privileges and
Immunities of the Trustee

Except as otherwise stated expressly to the contrary
herein, I give and grant to the said Trustee (and to the duly
appointed successor Trustee when acting as such) the power to
do everything he deems advisable with respect to the administration of each trust required to be established under this,
my last will and testament, even though such powers would not
be authorized or appropriate for the Trustee under statutory
or other rules of law. By way of illustration and not in
limitation of the generality of the foregoing grant of power
and authority of the Trustee, I give and grant to him plenary
power as follows:

(a) To exercise all those powers authorized to fidu-
ciaries under the provisions of the Tennessee Code Annotated,
Sections 35-616 to 35-618, inclusive, including any amendments
thereto in effect at the time of my death, and the same are
expressly referred to and incorporated herein by reference.

(b) Plenary power is granted to the Trustee, not only
to relieve him from seeking judicial instruction, but to the
extent that the Trustee deems it to be prudent, to encourage
determinations freely to be made in favor of persons who are
the current income beneficiaries. In such instances the rights
of all subsequent beneficiaries are subordinate, and the
Trustee shall not be answerable to any subsequent beneficiary
for anything done or omitted in favor of a current income
beneficiary, but no current income beneficiary may compel any
such favorable or preferential treatment. Without in anywise
minimizing or impairing the scope of this declaration of
intent, it includes investment policy, exercise of discre-
tionary power to pay or apply principal and income, and
determination of principal and income questions;

(c) It shall be lawful for the Trustee to apply any sum
that is payable to or for the benefit of a minor (or any other
person who in the judgment of the Trustee, is incapable of
making proper disposition thereof) by payments in discharge
of the costs and expenses of educating, maintaining and sup-
porting said beneficiary, or to make payment to anyone with
whom said beneficiary resides or who has the care or custody

of the beneficiary, temporarily or permanently, all without intervention of any guardian or like fiduciary. The receipt of anyone to whom payment is so authorized to be made shall be a complete discharge of the Trustee without obligation on his part to see to the further application thereof, and without regard to other resources that the beneficiary may have, or the duty of any other person to support the beneficiary;

(d) In dealing with the Trustee, no grantee, pledgee, vendee, mortgagee, lessee or other transferee of the trust properties, or any part thereof, shall be bound to inquire with respect to the purpose or necessity of any such disposition or to see to the application of any consideration therefor paid to the Trustee.

ITEM XIII
Concerning the Trustee
And the Executor

(a) If at any time the Trustee shall have reasonable doubt as to his power, authority or duty in the administration of any trust herein created, it shall be lawful for the Trustee to obtain the advice and counsel of reputable legal counsel without resorting to the courts for instructions; and the Trustee shall be fully absolved from all liability and damage or detriment to the various trust estates or any beneficiary thereunder by reason of anything done, suffered or omitted pursuant to advice of said counsel given and obtained in good faith, provided that nothing contained herein shall be construed to prohibit or prevent the Trustee in all proper cases from applying to a court of competent jurisdiction for instructions in the administration of the trust assets in lieu of obtaining advice of counsel.

(b) In managing, investing, and controlling the various trust estates, the Trustee shall exercise the judgment and care under the circumstances then prevailing, which men of prudence, discretion and judgment exercise in the management of their own affairs, not in regard to speculation, but in regard to the permanent disposition of their funds, considering the probable income as well as the probable safety of their capital, and, in addition, the purchasing power of income distribution to beneficiaries.

(c) My Trustee (as well as my Executor) shall be entitled to reasonable and adequate compensation for the fiduciary services rendered by him.

(d) My Executor and his successor Executor shall have the same rights, privileges, powers and immunities herein granted to my Trustee wherever appropriate.

(e) In referring to any fiduciary hereunder, for purposes of construction, masculine pronouns may include a corporate fiduciary and neutral pronouns may include an individual fiduciary.

ITEM XIV
Law Against Perpetuities

(a) Having in mind the rule against perpetuities, I direct that (notwithstanding anything contained to the contrary in this last will and testament) each trust created under this will (except such trusts as have heretofore vested in compliance with such rule or law) shall end, unless sooner terminated under other provisions of this will, twenty-one (21) years after the death of the last survivor of such of the beneficiaries hereunder as are living at the time of my death; and thereupon that the property held in trust shall be distributed free of all trust to the persons then entitled to receive the income and/or principal therefrom, in the proportion in which they are then entitled to receive such income.

(b) Notwithstanding anything else contained in this will to the contrary, I direct that if any distribution under this will becomes payable to a person for whom the Trustee is then administering a trust created hereunder for the benefit of such person, such distribution shall be made to such trust and not to the beneficiary outright, and the funds so passing to such trust shall become a part thereof as corpus and be administered and distributed to the same extent and purpose as if such funds had been a part of such trust at its inception.

ITEM XV
Payment of Estate and
Inheritance Taxes

Notwithstanding the provisions of ITEM X herein, I authorize my Executor to use such sums received by my estate

after my death and resulting from my personal services as
identified in ITEM X as he deems necessary and advisable in
order to pay the taxes referred to in ITEM I of my said will.

IN WITNESS WHEREOF, I, the said ELVIS A. PRESLEY, do
hereunto set my hand and seal in the presence of two (2)
competent witnesses, and in their presence do publish and
declare this instrument to be my Last Will and Testament, this
_3_ day of __March__ , 1977.

Elvis A Presley
ELVIS A. PRESLEY

The foregoing instrument, consisting of this and eleven
(11) preceding typewritten pages, was signed, sealed, published and declared by ELVIS A. PRESLEY, the Testator, to be
his Last Will and Testament, in our presence, and we, at his
request and in his presence and in the presence of each other,
have hereunto subscribed our names as witnesses, this _3_ day
of __March__ , 1977, at Memphis, Tennessee.

_____ residing at _____

_____ residing at _____

STATE OF TENNESSEE)
COUNTY OF SHELBY   )

_____ and _____ , after being
first duly sworn, make oath or affirm that the foregoing Last
Will and Testament was signed by ELVIS A. PRESLEY and for and
at that time acknowledged, published and declared by him to be
his Last Will and Testament, in the sight and presence of us,
the undersigned, who at his request and in his sight and
presence, and in the sight and presence of each other, have
subscribed our names as attesting witnesses on the _3_ day of
__March__ , 1977, and we further make oath or affirm that the
Testator was of sound mind and disposing memory and not acting
under fraud, menace or undue influence of any person, and was
more than eighteen (18) years of age; and that each of the
attesting witnesses is more than eighteen (18) years of age.

_____

_____

March   SWORN TO AND SUBSCRIBED before me this 3 day of
March , 1977.

                                          _____

                                          NOTARY PUBLIC

My commission expires:

_____

Admitted to Probate and Ordered Recorded August 22, 1977

                                          JOSEPH W. EVANS, JUDGE

Recorded August 22, 1977
B. J. DUNAVANT, CLERK
BY: Jan Scott, D. C.

LAST WILL AND TESTAMENT
Of
CLARK GABLE

I, CLARK GABLE, being of sound and disposing mind, and free from fraud, duress, menace or undue influence, do hereby make, declare and publish this, my Last Will and Testament.

FIRST: I hereby expressly revoke any and all former Wills and Codicils thereto heretofore made by me.

SECOND: I hereby declare that I am married to Kathleen G. Gable and that I have no children.

THIRD: I direct that all of my just debts, expenses of last illness and expenses of burial be first paid.

FOURTH: I give, devise and bequeath to JOSEPHINE DILLON, my former wife, that certain real property situate in the County of Los Angeles, State of California, known as 12746 Landale, North Hollywood, California, and more particularly described as follows:

The West fifty (50) feet of the East one hundred (100) feet of Lot 9, Tract 5588, as per map recorded in Book 59, page 49, of Maps, in the office of the Recorder of said County.

FIFTH: All of the rest, residue and remainder of my estate, real, personal or mixed, I give, devise and bequeath to my beloved wife, KATHLEEN G. GABLE.

SIXTH: I direct that all succession, inheritance or other death taxes or duties (by whatever name called) imposed upon or in relation to any property owned by me at the time of my death or required to be included in my gross estate under the provisions of any tax law shall be paid out of the residue of my estate without any charge therefor against any specific bequest or devise hereunder or against any assets not included in my probate estate.

SEVENTH: I hereby generally and expressly disinherit each and all persons whomsoever claiming to be and who may be my heirs at law, and each and all persons whomsoever who, if I died intestate, would be entitled to any part of my estate, except those herein provided for. If any devisee, legatee or beneficiary under this Will, or any person claiming under or through any devisee, legatee or beneficiary, or any other person who, if I died wholly or partially intestate, would be entitled to share in my estate, shall in any manner whatsoever, directly or indirectly, contest this Will or attack or oppose, or in any manner seek to impair or invalidate any provision hereof, or shall endeavor to succeed to any part of my estate otherwise than through this Will, then in each of the above mentioned cases I hereby bequeath to such person or persons the sum of One ($1.00) Dollar only, and all other bequests, devises and interest in this Will given to such person or persons shall be forfeited and become a part of the residue of my estate.

EIGHTH: I hereby appoint my beloved wife, KATHLEEN G. GABLE, to serve as executrix of my estate, without bond.

IN WITNESS WHEREOF, I have hereunto set my hand this 19 day of September , 1955.

_____

The foregoing instrument, consisting of three pages, including the page signed by the testator, was on the date hereof by the said CLARK GABLE, subscribed, published and declared to be his Last Will and Testament in the presence of us, and each of us, who at his request and in his presence, and in the presence of each other, have signed the same as witnesses thereto.

_____ Residing at _____

                                 _____

_____ Residing at _____

                                 _____

_____ Residing at _____

                                 _____

Last Will and Testament
of
LIBERACE

I, LIBERACE, also sometimes known as WALTER VALENTINO LIBERACE, LEE LIBERACE and WLADSIU VALENTINO LIBERACE, domiciled in Las Vegas, Nevada, being of sound and disposing mind and memory, do hereby make, publish and declare this to be my LAST WILL AND TESTAMENT, and hereby revoke any and all Wills and Codicils at any time heretofore made by me.

FIRST: <u>MARITAL AND FAMILY STATUS</u>

I declare that I am unmarried and have no living issue.

SECOND: <u>BEQUESTS</u>

2.1 <u>Bequest to Trust</u>. I give, devise and bequeath my entire estate, both real and personal, to JOEL R. STROTE, as Trustee, or any successor Trustee of the trust designated as ''THE LIBERACE REVOCABLE TRUST'' established earlier this day, of which I am the Grantor and he is the original Trustee. I direct that my estate shall be added to, administered and distributed as part of that trust, according to the terms of that trust and any amendments made to it before my death. To the extent permitted by law, it is not my intention to create a separate trust by this Will or to subject the trust or the property added to it by this Will to the jurisdiction of the Probate Court.

2.2 <u>Incorporation by Reference</u>. If the disposition in Section 2.1 is not operative or is invalid for any reason, or if the trust referred to in that Section fails or has been revoked, then I hereby incorporate by reference the terms of that trust, including any amendments thereto, and I give, devise and bequeath my estate to the Trustee named in the trust as Trustee, to be held, administered and distributed as provided in that instrument.

Testator Initials_____

THIRD: EXECUTORS

    3.1 Appointment of Executor. I nominate, constitute and appoint JOEL R. STROTE as Executor of this Will. The term ''my Executor'' as used in this Will shall include any personal representative of my estate.

    3.2 Waiver of Bond. No bond shall be required of any Executor nominated in this Will.

    3.3 Appointment of Ancillary Fiduciaries. Should ancillary administration be necessary or advantageous in any jurisdiction and should my Executor be unable and/or unwilling to act as my ancillary fiduciary, I nominate, constitute and appoint as ancillary fiduciary such qualified person or trust institution as my Executor shall from time to time designate (with retained right of removal) in a writing filed in the court having ancillary jurisdiction. Furthermore, all my ancillary fiduciaries shall at all times be subject to the directions of my Executor and the residuary estate of each ancillary administration shall be transmitted to my Executor as promptly as possible.

    3.4 Election of Simplified Unsupervised Administration. If independent administration without certain court proceeding and supervision is to any extent permitted under the laws of any jurisdiction in which any part of my estate is being administered, I hereby elect such simplified mode(s) of administration and direct, to the greatest extent possible, settlement of my estate without the intervention of or accountings to any courts.

    3.5 General Powers. In addition to, and not in limitation of the Executor's common law and statutory powers, and without order or approval of any court, I give and grant to my Executor the rights and powers to take any action desirable for the complete administration of my estate, including the power to determine what property is covered by general descriptions contained in this Will, the power to sell, with or without notice, at either public or private sale, and to lease any property belonging to my estate, subject only to such confirmation of court as may be required by law.

Testator Initials_____

3.6 <u>Power Regarding Tax Returns</u>. My Executor is authorized to file an income tax return for me and to pay all or
any portion of the taxes due thereon. If any additional
assessment shall be made on account of any income tax return
which I have filed, my Executor is authorized to pay the
additional assessment. The exercise of authority hereunder by
my Executor shall be conclusive and binding on all persons.

3.7 <u>Power to Make Tax Elections</u>. My Executor has the
authority to make the following choices or elections:

(a) Choose the methods of payment of federal estate
taxes or state estate or inheritance taxes.

(b) Determine whether any or all of the expenses of administration of my estate shall be used as federal estate tax
deductions or as federal income tax deductions. No beneficiary
under this Will shall have any right to recoupment or restoration of any loss the beneficiary suffers as a result of the
use of such deduction for one or the other of these purposes.

(c) Exercise any other options or elections afforded by
the tax law of the United States or of any other jurisdiction.
My Executor may exercise this authority in my Executor's sole
discretion, regardless of any other provisions in this Will or
the effect on any other provisions of this Will or the effect
on any person interested in my estate. No beneficiary under
this Will shall be entitled to a compensating adjustment, even
though the exercise of these tax powers affects the size or
composition of my estate or of any disposition under this
Will. The determination of my Executor with respect to the
exercise of the election shall be conclusive upon all affected
persons.

3.8 <u>Power to Employ</u>. My Executor may employ and
compensate from my estate accountants, brokers, attorneys,
investment advisors, custodians and others whose services are,
in my Executor's discretion, necessary or convenient to the
administration of the estate created herein. I request, but do
not direct, that my Executor employ FRANK DI BELLA, of
Whittier, California, as the accountant for my estate. I make
this request because it is my belief that said accountant is

Testator Initials_____

well qualified to act in that capacity, and I have the utmost confidence in his abilities in that regard. My Executor is expressly authorized to employ and compensate my Executor or any firm with which my Executor may be associated to perform any services that are in my Executor's opinion necessary or convenient to the administration of my estate.

3.9 <u>Continuance of Business</u>. I further authorize my Executor either to continue the operation of any business belonging to my estate for such time and in such manner as my Executor may deem advisable and for the best interests of my estate, or to sell or liquidate the business at such time and on such terms as my Executor may deem advisable and for the best interests of my estate. Any such operation, sale, or liquidation by my Executor in good faith, shall be at the risk of my estate and without liability on the part of my Executor for any resulting losses.

3.10 <u>Power to Transact with Trusts</u>. My Executor is hereby authorized to purchase any property, and to make loans and advances to, or otherwise deal with, the Trustee of any trust, including, but not limited to, trusts wherein the Executor and Trustee shall be the same parties.

FOURTH: <u>TESTAMENTARY DECLARATIONS</u>

4.1 <u>Non-exercise of Powers of Appointment</u>. I refrain from exercising any testamentary power of appointment that I may have at the time of my death.

4.2 <u>Confirmation of Gifts</u>. I hereby ratify and confirm all gifts made by me prior to my death, and I direct that none of those gifts should be deemed or construed to be an advancement to any beneficiary nor shall any gift be taken into account in the settlement of my estate.

FIFTH: <u>MISCELLANEOUS</u>

5.1 <u>Incontestability</u>. If any beneficiary under this Will in any manner, directly or indirectly, contests or attacks this Will or any of its provisions, any share or interest in my estate given to the contesting beneficiary

Testator Initials_____

under this Will is revoked and shall be disposed of in the same manner provided herein as if the contesting beneficiary had predeceased me.

5.2 <u>Tax Contribution</u>. I direct that every specific and general gift, devise or bequest given under this Will or any Codicil hereto shall be delivered free of all estate and inheritance taxes and that such taxes be paid out of the residue of my estate. I further direct that no legatee, devisee or beneficiary hereunder, or beneficiary under any of my life insurance policies, or any surviving joint tenant, or any trustee of any private trust of mine which shall be in existence at the time of my death, shall be called upon to make any contributions toward the payment of any estate or inheritance taxes.

5.3 <u>Severability</u>. If any part or parts of this Will shall be invalid, illegal, or inoperative, it is my intention that the remaining parts shall stand and be effective and operative.

5.4 <u>Gender and Number</u>. As used in this Will, the masculine, feminine or neuter gender, and the singular or plural number, shall each be deemed to include the others whenever the context so indicates.

5.5 <u>Headings</u>. The headings, titles and subtitles in this Will have been inserted for convenient reference, and shall be ignored in its construction.

IN WITNESS WHEREOF, I have hereunto set my hand this 22nd day of January, 1987.

_____
LIBERACE

On the date last above written, LIBERACE declared to us that the foregoing instrument, consisting of five (5) pages, including the affidavit signed by us as witnesses, was

Testator Initials_____

his Will and requested us to act as witnesses to it. He thereupon signed this Will in our presence all of us being present at the same time. We now, at his request, in his presence, and in the presence of each other, subscribe our names as witnesses.

_____ residing at _____

_____

_____ residing at _____

_____

_____ residing at _____

_____

STATE OF CALIFORNIA   )
                      ss.:
COUNTY OF LOS ANGELES)

    Then and there personally appeared the within named _____, _____, and _____who being duly sworn, depose and say:

    That they witnessed the execution of the within Will of the within named Testator, LIBERACE, that the Testator subscribed the Will and declared the same to be his Will in their presence; that they thereafter subscribed the same as witnesses in the presence of the Testator and in the presence of each other and at the request of the Testator; that the Testator at the time of the execution appeared to be of full age and of sound mind and memory and under no constraint; and that they make this Affidavit at the request of the Testator.

_____

_____

_____

SUBSCRIBED and SWORN to before me this
22nd day of January, 1987.

_____
    NOTARY PUBLIC

Testator Initials_____

Appendix B
Important Forms

Form **706**	**United States Estate (and Generation-Skipping Transfer)**	
(Rev. August 1993)	**Tax Return**	OMB No. 1545-0015
Department of the Treasury Internal Revenue Service	Estate of a citizen or resident of the United States (see separate instructions). To be filed for decedents dying after October 8, 1990. For Paperwork Reduction Act Notice, see page 1 of the instructions.	Expires 12-31-95

Part 1.—Decedent and Executor

1a Decedent's first name and middle initial (and maiden name, if any)	1b Decedent's last name	2 Decedent's social security no.
3a Domicile at time of death (county and state, or foreign country)	3b Year domicile established　4 Date of birth	5 Date of death
6a Name of executor (see instructions)	6b Executor's address (number and street including apartment or suite no. or rural route; city, town, or post office; state; and ZIP code)	
6c Executor's social security number (see instructions)		
7a Name and location of court where will was probated or estate administered		7b Case number

8　If decedent died testate, check here ▶ ☐ and attach a certified copy of the will.　9　If Form 4768 is attached, check here ▶ ☐

10　If Schedule R-1 is attached, check here ▶ ☐

Part 2.—Tax Computation

1	Total gross estate (from Part 5, Recapitulation, page 3, item 10)	**1**		
2	Total allowable deductions (from Part 5, Recapitulation, page 3, item 20)	**2**		
3	Taxable estate (subtract line 2 from line 1)	**3**		
4	Adjusted taxable gifts (total taxable gifts (within the meaning of section 2503) made by the decedent after December 31, 1976, other than gifts that are includible in decedent's gross estate (section 2001(b))	**4**		
5	Add lines 3 and 4	**5**		
6	Tentative tax on the amount on line 5 from Table A in the instructions	**6**		
7a	If line 5 exceeds $10,000,000, enter the lesser of line 5 or $21,040,000. If line 5 is $10,000,000 or less, skip lines 7a and 7b and enter -0- on line 7c.	**7a**		
b	Subtract $10,000,000 from line 7a	**7b**		
c	Enter 5% (.05) of line 7b	**7c**		
8	Total tentative tax (add lines 6 and 7c)	**8**		
9	Total gift tax payable with respect to gifts made by the decedent after December 31, 1976. Include gift taxes by the decedent's spouse for such spouse's share of split gifts (section 2513) only if the decedent was the donor of these gifts and they are includible in the decedent's gross estate (see instructions)	**9**		
10	Gross estate tax (subtract line 9 from line 8)	**10**		
11	Maximum unified credit against estate tax	**11**　192,800	00	
12	Adjustment to unified credit. (This adjustment may not exceed $6,000. See page 6 of the instructions.)	**12**		
13	Allowable unified credit (subtract line 12 from line 11)	**13**		
14	Subtract line 13 from line 10 (but do not enter less than zero)	**14**		
15	Credit for state death taxes. Do not enter more than line 14. Compute the credit by using the amount on line 3 less $60,000. See Table B in the instructions and **attach credit evidence** (see instructions)	**15**		
16	Subtract line 15 from line 14	**16**		
17	Credit for Federal gift taxes on pre-1977 gifts (section 2012) (attach computation)	**17**		
18	Credit for foreign death taxes (from Schedule(s) P). (Attach Form(s) 706CE)	**18**		
19	Credit for tax on prior transfers (from Schedule Q)	**19**		
20	Total (add lines 17, 18, and 19)	**20**		
21	Net estate tax (subtract line 20 from line 16)	**21**		
22	Generation-skipping transfer taxes (from Schedule R, Part 2, line 10)	**22**		
23	Section 4980A increased estate tax (from Schedule S, Part I, line 17) (see instructions) . . .	**23**		
24	Total transfer taxes (add lines 21, 22, and 23)	**24**		
25	Prior payments. Explain in an attached statement	**25**		
26	United States Treasury bonds redeemed in payment of estate tax .	**26**		
27	Total (add lines 25 and 26)	**27**		
28	Balance due (or overpayment) (subtract line 27 from line 24)	**28**		

Under penalties of perjury, I declare that I have examined this return, including accompanying schedules and statements, and to the best of my knowledge and belief, it is true, correct, and complete. Declaration of preparer other than the executor is based on all information of which preparer has any knowledge.

Signature(s) of executor(s)　　　　　　　　　　　　　　　　　　　Date

Signature of preparer other than executor　　　Address (and ZIP code)　　　Date

Cat. No. 20548R

Form 706 (Rev. 8-93)

Estate of:

Part 3.—Elections by the Executor

Please check the "Yes" or "No" box for each question.	Yes	No
1 Do you elect alternate valuation?		
2 Do you elect special use valuation? . . . . If "Yes," you must complete and attach Schedule A–1		
3 Do you elect to pay the taxes in installments as described in section 6166? . . . . If "Yes," you must attach the additional information described in the instructions.		
4 Do you elect to postpone the part of the taxes attributable to a reversionary or remainder interest as described in section 6163?		

Part 4.—General Information (Note: *Please attach the necessary supplemental documents. You must attach the death certificate.*)

Authorization to receive confidential tax information under Regulations section 601.504(b)(2)(i), to act as the estate's representative before the Internal Revenue Service, and to make written or oral presentations on behalf of the estate if return prepared by an attorney, accountant, or enrolled agent for the executor:

Name of representative (print or type)	State	Address (number, street, and room or suite no., city, state, and ZIP code)

I declare that I am the ☐ attorney/ ☐ certified public accountant/ ☐ enrolled agent (you must check the applicable box) for the executor and prepared this return for the executor. I am not under suspension or disbarment from practice before the Internal Revenue Service and am qualified to practice in the state shown above.

Signature	CAF number	Date	Telephone number

1   Death certificate number and issuing authority (attach a copy of the death certificate to this return).

2   Decedent's business or occupation. If retired, check here ▶ ☐ and state decedent's former business or occupation.

3   Marital status of the decedent at time of death:
   ☐ Married
   ☐ Widow or widower—Name, SSN, and date of death of deceased spouse ▶ ....
   ....
   ☐ Single
   ☐ Legally separated
   ☐ Divorced—Date divorce decree became final ▶

4a Surviving spouse's name	4b Social security number	4c Amount received (see instructions)

5   Individuals (other than the surviving spouse), trusts, or other estates who receive benefits from the estate (do not include charitable beneficiaries shown in Schedule O) (see instructions). For Privacy Act Notice (applicable to individual beneficiaries only), see the instructions for Form 1040.

Name of individual, trust, or estate receiving $5,000 or more	Identifying number	Relationship to decedent	Amount (see instructions)

All unascertainable beneficiaries and those who receive less than $5,000 . . . . ▶

Total . . . .

(Continued on next page)

Page 2

Form 706 (Rev. 8-93)

Estate of:

SCHEDULE A—Real Estate

(For jointly owned property that must be disclosed on Schedule E, see the instructions for Schedule E.)

(Real estate that is part of a sole proprietorship should be shown on Schedule F. Real estate that is included in the gross estate under section 2035, 2036, 2037, or 2038 should be shown on Schedule G. Real estate that is included in the gross estate under section 2041 should be shown on Schedule H.)

(If you elect section 2032A valuation, you must complete Schedule A and Schedule A-1.)

Item number	Description	Alternate valuation date	Alternate value	Value at date of death
1				
	Total from continuation schedule(s) (or additional sheet(s)) attached to this schedule . .			
	TOTAL. (Also enter on Part 5, Recapitulation, page 3, at item 1.)			

(If more space is needed, attach the continuation schedule from the end of this package or additional sheets of the same size.)

(See the instructions on the reverse side.)

Schedule A—Page 4

Form 709
(Rev. November 1993)

Department of the Treasury
Internal Revenue Service

United States Gift (and Generation-Skipping Transfer) Tax Return

(Section 6019 of the Internal Revenue Code) (For gifts made after December 31, 1991)

Calendar year 19 ....

▶ **See separate instructions. For Privacy Act Notice, see the Instructions for Form 1040.**

OMB No. 1545-0020
Expires 5-31-96

1 Donor's first name and middle initial	2 Donor's last name	3 Donor's social security number

4 Address (number, street, and apartment number)	5 Legal residence (Domicile) (county and state)

6 City, state, and ZIP code	7 Citizenship

Part 1—General Information

		Yes	No
8	If the donor died during the year, check here ▶ ☐ and enter date of death.............., 19		
9	If you received an extension of time to file this Form 709, check here ▶ ☐ and attach the Form 4868, 2688, 2350, or extension letter		
10	Enter the total number of separate donees listed on Schedule A—count each person only once . . . . ▶		
11a	Have you (the donor) previously filed a Form 709 (or 709-A) for any other year? If the answer is "No," do not complete line 11b .		
11b	If the answer to line 11a is "Yes," has your address changed since you last filed Form 709 (or 709-A)?		

12 Gifts by husband or wife to third parties.—Do you consent to have the gifts (including generation-skipping transfers) made by you and by your spouse to third parties during the calendar year considered as made one-half by each of you? (See instructions.) (If the answer is "Yes," the following information must be furnished and your spouse must sign the consent shown below. **If the answer is "No," skip lines 13–18 and go to Schedule A.**) .

13 Name of consenting spouse	14 SSN	

15	Were you married to one another during the entire calendar year? (see instructions)		
16	If the answer to 15 is "No," check whether ☐ married ☐ divorced or ☐ widowed, and give date (see instructions) ▶		
17	Will a gift tax return for this calendar year be filed by your spouse?		

18 **Consent of Spouse**—I consent to have the gifts (and generation-skipping transfers) made by me and by my spouse to third parties during the calendar year considered as made one-half by each of us. We are both aware of the joint and several liability for tax created by the execution of this consent.

Consenting spouse's signature ▶   Date ▶

Part 2—Tax Computation

1	Enter the amount from Schedule A, Part 3, line 15	1	
2	Enter the amount from Schedule B, line 3	2	
3	Total taxable gifts (add lines 1 and 2)	3	
4	Tax computed on amount on line 3 (see Table for Computing Tax in separate instructions). . .	4	
5	Tax computed on amount on line 2 (see Table for Computing Tax in separate instructions). . .	5	
6	Balance (subtract line 5 from line 4)	6	
7	Maximum unified credit (nonresident aliens, see instructions)	7	192,800 | 00
8	Enter the unified credit against tax allowable for all prior periods (from Sch. B, line 1, col. C) . .	8	
9	Balance (subtract line 8 from line 7)	9	
10	Enter 20% (.20) of the amount allowed as a specific exemption for gifts made after September 8, 1976, and before January 1, 1977 (see instructions)	10	
11	Balance (subtract line 10 from line 9)	11	
12	Unified credit (enter the smaller of line 6 or line 11)	12	
13	Credit for foreign gift taxes (see instructions)	13	
14	Total credits (add lines 12 and 13)	14	
15	Balance (subtract line 14 from line 6) (do not enter less than zero)	15	
16	Generation-skipping transfer taxes (from Schedule C, Part 3, col. H, total)	16	
17	Total tax (add lines 15 and 16)	17	
18	Gift and generation-skipping transfer taxes prepaid with extension of time to file	18	
19	If line 18 is less than line 17, enter BALANCE DUE (see instructions)	19	
20	If line 18 is greater than line 17, enter AMOUNT TO BE REFUNDED	20	

Under penalties of perjury, I declare that I have examined this return, including any accompanying schedules and statements, and to the best of my knowledge and belief it is true, correct, and complete. Declaration of preparer (other than donor) is based on all information of which preparer has any knowledge.

Donor's signature ▶   Date ▶

Preparer's signature
(other than donor) ▶   Date ▶

Preparer's address
(other than donor) ▶

Attach check or money order here.

For Paperwork Reduction Act Notice, see page 1 of the separate instructions for this form.   Cat. No. 16783M   Form **709** (Rev. 11-93)

Form 709 (Rev. 11-93)   Page **2**

| SCHEDULE A | **Computation of Taxable Gifts** |

Part 1—Gifts Subject Only to Gift Tax. *Gifts less political organization, medical, and educational exclusions—see instructions*

A Item number	B • Donee's name and address • Relationship to donor (if any) • Description of gift • If the gift was made by means of a trust, enter trust's identifying number and attach a copy of the trust instrument • If the gift was of securities, give CUSIP number	C Donor's adjusted basis of gift	D Date of gift	E Value at date of gift
1				

Part 2—Gifts That are Direct Skips and are Subject to Both Gift Tax and Generation-Skipping Transfer Tax. You must list the gifts in chronological order. *Gifts less political organization, medical, and educational exclusions—see instructions. (Also list here direct skips that are subject only to the GST tax at this time as the result of the termination of an "estate tax inclusion period." See instructions.)*

A Item number	B • Donee's name and address • Relationship to donor (if any) • Description of gift • If the gift was made by means of a trust, enter trust's identifying number and attach a copy of the trust instrument • If the gift was of securities, give CUSIP number	C Donor's adjusted basis of gift	D Date of gift	E Value at date of gift
1				

Part 3—Taxable Gift Reconciliation

1	Total value of gifts of donor (add column E of Parts 1 and 2)	**1**	
2	One-half of items ....attributable to spouse (see instructions)	**2**	
3	Balance (subtract line 2 from line 1)	**3**	
4	Gifts of spouse to be included (from Schedule A, Part 3, line 2 of spouse's return—see instructions) . .	**4**	
	If any of the gifts included on this line are also subject to the generation-skipping transfer tax, check here ▶ ☐ and enter those gifts also on Schedule C, Part 1.		
5	Total gifts (add lines 3 and 4)	**5**	
6	Total annual exclusions for gifts listed on Schedule A (including line 4, above) (see instructions) . . .	**6**	
7	Total included amount of gifts (subtract line 6 from line 5)	**7**	

Deductions (see instructions)

8	Gifts of interests to spouse for which a marital deduction will be claimed, based on items ....of Schedule A	**8**		
9	Exclusions attributable to gifts on line 8	**9**		
10	Marital deduction—subtract line 9 from line 8	**10**		
11	Charitable deduction, based on items ....to ....less exclusions	**11**		
12	Total deductions—add lines 10 and 11		**12**	
13	Subtract line 12 from line 7		**13**	
14	Generation-skipping transfer taxes payable with this Form 709 (from Schedule C, Part 3, col. H, Total) .		**14**	
15	Taxable gifts (add lines 13 and 14). Enter here and on line 1 of the Tax Computation on page 1 . . .		**15**	

(If more space is needed, attach additional sheets of same size.)

Form 709 (Rev. 11-93)

SCHEDULE A   Computation of Taxable Gifts *(continued)*

16 Terminable Interest (QTIP) Marital Deduction. (See instructions for line 8 of Schedule A.)

If a trust (or other property) meets the requirements of qualified terminable interest property under section 2523(f), and

   a. The trust (or other property) is listed on Schedule A, and

   b. The value of the trust (or other property) is entered in whole or in part as a deduction on line 8, Part 3 of Schedule A,

then the donor shall be deemed to have made an election to have such trust (or other property) treated as qualified terminable interest property under section 2523(f).

   If less than the entire value of the trust (or other property) that the donor has included in Part 1 of Schedule A is entered as a deduction on line 8, the donor shall be considered to have made an election only as to a fraction of the trust (or other property). The numerator of this fraction is equal to the amount of the trust (or other property) deducted on line 10 of Part 3. The denominator is equal to the total value of the trust (or other property) listed in Part 1 of Schedule A.

   If you make the QTIP election (see instructions for line 8 of Schedule A), the terminable interest property involved will be included in your spouse's gross estate upon his or her death (section 2044). If your spouse disposes (by gift or otherwise) of all or part of the qualifying life income interest, he or she will be considered to have made a transfer of the entire property that is subject to the gift tax (see Transfer of Certain Life Estates on page 3 of the instructions).

17 Election out of QTIP Treatment of Annuities

☐ ◄ Check here if you elect under section 2523(f)(6) **NOT** to treat as qualified terminable interest property any joint and survivor annuities that are reported on Schedule A and would otherwise be treated as qualified terminable interest property under section 2523(f). (See instructions.)
Enter the item numbers (from Schedule A) for the annuities for which you are making this election ►

SCHEDULE B   Gifts From Prior Periods

If you answered "Yes" on line 11a of page 1, Part 1, see the instructions for completing Schedule B. If you answered "No," skip to the Tax Computation on page 1 (or Schedule C, if applicable).

A Calendar year or calendar quarter (see instructions)	B Internal Revenue office where prior return was filed	C Amount of unified credit against gift tax for periods after December 31, 1976	D Amount of specific exemption for prior periods ending before January 1, 1977	E Amount of taxable gifts

1 Totals for prior periods (without adjustment for reduced specific exemption)	**1**			
2 Amount, if any, by which total specific exemption, line 1, column D, is more than $30,000			**2**	
3 Total amount of taxable gifts for prior periods (add amount, column E, line 1, and amount, if any, on line 2). (Enter here and on line 2 of the Tax Computation on page 1.)			**3**	

(If more space is needed, attach additional sheets of same size.)

Form 709 (Rev. 11-93)   Page **4**

SCHEDULE C   **Computation of Generation-Skipping Transfer Tax**

Note: *Inter vivos direct skips that are completely excluded by the GST exemption must still be fully reported (including value and exemptions claimed) on Schedule C.*

Part 1—Generation-Skipping Transfers

A Item No. (from Schedule A, Part 2, col. A)	B Value (from Schedule A, Part 2, col. E)	C Split Gifts (enter ½ of col. B) (see instructions)	D Subtract col. C from col. B	E Nontaxable portion of transfer	F Net Transfer (subtract col. E from col. D)
1					
2					
3					
4					
5					
6					

If you elected gift splitting and your spouse was required to file a separate Form 709 (see the instructions for "Split Gifts"), you must enter all of the gifts shown on Schedule A, Part 2, of your spouse's Form 709 here. In column C, enter the item number of each gift in the order it appears in column A of your spouse's Schedule A, Part 2. We have preprinted the prefix "S-" to distinguish your spouse's item numbers from your own when you complete column A of Schedule C, Part 3. In column D, for each gift, enter the amount reported in column C, Schedule C, Part 1, of your spouse's Form 709.	Split gifts from spouse's Form 709 (enter item number)	Value included from spouse's Form 709	Nontaxable portion of transfer	Net transfer (subtract col. E from col. D)
	S-			
	S-			
	S-			
	S-			
	S-			
	S-			
	S-			
	S-			

Part 2—GST Exemption Reconciliation (Code section 2631) and Section 2652(a)(3) Election

Check box ▶ ☐   if you are making a section 2652(a)(3) (special QTIP) election (see instructions)

Enter the item numbers (from Schedule A) of the gifts for which you are making this election ▶ ....

1	Maximum allowable exemption	**1**	$1,000,000
2	Total exemption used for periods before filing this return	**2**	
3	Exemption available for this return (subtract line 2 from line 1)	**3**	
4	Exemption claimed on this return (from Part 3, col. C total, below)	**4**	
5	Exemption allocated to transfers not shown on Part 3, below. You must attach a Notice of Allocation. (See instructions.)	**5**	
6	Add lines 4 and 5	**6**	
7	Exemption available for future transfers (subtract line 6 from line 3)	**7**	

Part 3—Tax Computation

A Item No. (from Schedule C, Part 1)	B Net transfer (from Schedule C, Part 1, col. F)	C GST Exemption Allocated	D Divide col. C by col. B	E Inclusion Ratio (subtract col. D from 1.000)	F Maximum Estate Tax Rate	G Applicable Rate (multiply col. E by col. F)	H Generation-Skipping Transfer Tax (multiply col. B by col. G)
1					55% (.55)		
2					55% (.55)		
3					55% (.55)		
4					55% (.55)		
5					55% (.55)		
6					55% (.55)		
					55% (.55)		
					55% (.55)		
					55% (.55)		

Total exemption claimed. Enter here and on line 4, Part 2, above. May not exceed line 3, Part 2, above	**Total generation-skipping transfer tax.** Enter here, on line 14 of Schedule A, Part 3, and on line 16 of the Tax Computation on page 1	

(If more space is needed, attach additional sheets of same size.)   *U.S. Government Printing Office: 1995 — 387-085/00374

Form **709-A**

(Rev. July 1993)

Department of the Treasury
Internal Revenue Service

United States Short Form Gift Tax Return

(For "Privacy Act" notice, see the Form 1040 instructions)

Calendar year 19.........

OMB No. 1545-0021

Expires 5-31-96

1 Donor's first name and middle initial	2 Donor's last name	3 Donor's social security number

4 Address (number, street, and apartment number)	5 Legal residence (domicile)

6 City, state, and ZIP code	7 Citizenship

8 Did you file any gift tax returns for prior periods? . . . . ☐ Yes ☐ No

If "Yes," state when and where earlier returns were filed ▶

9 Name of consenting spouse	10 Consenting spouse's social security number

Note: *Do not use this form to report gifts of closely held stock. Instead, use Form 709.*

List of Gifts

(a) Donee's name and address and description of gift	(b) Donor's adjusted basis of gift	(c) Date of gift	(d) Value at date of gift

Consent

I consent to have the gifts made by my spouse to third parties during the calendar year considered as made one-half by each of us.

Consenting spouse's signature ▶

Date ▶

Under penalties of perjury, I declare that I have examined this return, and to the best of my knowledge and belief it is true, correct, and complete. Declaration of preparer (other than donor) is based on all information of which preparer has any knowledge.

Donor's signature ▶ ....

Date ▶ ....

Preparer's signature (other than donor's) ▶ ....

Date ▶ ....

Preparer's address (other than donor's) ▶

For Paperwork Reduction Act Notice, see the instructions on the reverse side of this form.   Cat. No. 10171G   Form **709-A** (Rev. 7-93)

Form **712**
(Rev. August 1994)
Department of the Treasury
Internal Revenue Service

Life Insurance Statement

OMB No. 1545-0022

Part I   **Decedent—Insured** (To Be Filed by the Executor With United States Estate Tax Return, Form 706 or Form 706-NA)

1 Decedent's first name and middle initial	2 Decedent's last name	3 Decedent's social security number (if known)	4 Date of death

5   Name and address of insurance company

6 Type of policy	7 Policy number

8 Owner's name. If decedent is not owner, attach copy of application.	9 Date issued	10 Assignor's name. Attach copy of assignment.	11 Date assigned

12 Value of the policy at the time of assignment	13 Amount of premium (see instructions)	14 Name of beneficiaries

15   Face amount of policy . . . . $

16   Indemnity benefits . . . . $

17   Additional insurance . . . . $

18   Other benefits. . . . . $

19   Principal of any indebtedness to the company that is deductible in determining net proceeds . . . $

20   Interest on indebtedness (line 19) accrued to date of death . . . . $

21   Amount of accumulated dividends . . . . $

22   Amount of post-mortem dividends . . . . $

23   Amount of returned premium . . . . $

24   Amount of proceeds if payable in one sum . . . . $

25   Value of proceeds as of date of death (if not payable in one sum) . . . . $

26   Policy provisions concerning deferred payments or installments.

     Note: *If other than lump-sum settlement is authorized for a surviving spouse, attach a copy of the insurance policy.*

27   Amount of installments . . . . $

28   Date of birth, sex, and name of any person the duration of whose life may measure the number of payments.

29   Amount applied by the insurance company as a single premium representing the purchase of installment benefits . . . . $

30   Basis (mortality table and rate of interest) used by insurer in valuing installment benefits.

31   Was the insured the annuitant or beneficiary of any annuity contract issued by the company? . . . .   ☐ **Yes**   ☐ **No**

32   Names of companies with which decedent carried other policies and amount of such policies if this information is disclosed by your records.

The undersigned officer of the above-named insurance company hereby certifies that this statement sets forth true and correct information.

Signature ▶   Title ▶   Date of Certification ▶

Instructions

Paperwork Reduction Act Notice.—We ask for the information on this form to carry out the Internal Revenue laws of the United States. You are required to give us the information. We need it to ensure that you are complying with these laws and to allow us to figure and collect the right amount of tax.

The time needed to complete and file this form will vary depending on individual circumstances. The estimated average time is:

Form	Recordkeeping	Preparing the form
712	18 hrs., 25 min.	18 min.

If you have comments concerning the accuracy of these time estimates or suggestions for making this form more simple, we would be happy to hear from you. You can write to both the IRS and the Office of

Management and Budget at the addresses listed in the instructions of the tax return with which this form is filed. **DO NOT** send the tax form to either of these offices. Instead, return it to the executor or representative who requested it.

Statement of insurer.—This statement must be made, on behalf of the insurance company that issued the policy, by an officer of the company having access to the records of the company. For purposes of this statement, a facsimile signature may be used in lieu of a manual signature and if used, shall be binding as a manual signature.

Separate statements.—File a separate Form 712 for each policy.

Line 13.—Report on line 13 the annual premium, not the cumulative premium to date of death. If death occurred after the end of the premium period, report the last annual premium.

Cat. No. 10170V   Form **712** (Rev. 8-94)

Form 712 (Rev. 8-94) Page **2**

Part II **Living Insured**
(File With United States Gift Tax Return, Form 709. May Be Filed With United States Estate Tax Return, Form 706 or Form 706-NA, Where Decedent Owned Insurance on Life of Another)

SECTION A—General Information

33 First name and middle initial of donor (or decedent)	**34** Last name	**35** Social security number

36 Date of gift for which valuation data submitted . . . . ▶	
37 Date of decedent's death for which valuation data submitted . . . . ▶	

SECTION B—Policy Information

38 Name of insured	**39** Sex	**40** Date of birth

41 Name and address of insurance company

42 Type of policy	**43** Policy number	**44** Face amount	**45** Issue date

46 Gross premium	**47** Frequency of payment

48 Assignee's name	**49** Date assigned

50 If irrevocable designation of beneficiary made, name of beneficiary	**51** Sex	**52** Date of birth, if known	**53** Date designated

54 If other than simple designation, quote in full. (Attach additional sheets if necessary.)

55 If policy is not paid up:
  a Interpolated terminal reserve on date of death, assignment, or irrevocable designation of beneficiary . . . .
  b Add proportion of gross premium paid beyond date of death, assignment, or irrevocable designation of beneficiary . . . .
  c Add adjustment on account of dividends to credit of policy . . . .
  d **Total** (add lines a, b, and c) . . . .
  e Outstanding indebtedness against policy . . . .
  f Net total value of the policy (for gift or estate tax purposes) (subtract line e from line d) . . .
56 If policy is either paid up or a single premium:
  a Total cost, on date of death, assignment, or irrevocable designation of beneficiary, of a single-premium policy on life of insured at attained age, for original face amount plus any additional paid-up insurance (additional face amount $ _____)

  (If a single-premium policy for the total face amount would not have been issued on the life of the insured as of the date specified, nevertheless, assume that such a policy could then have been purchased by the insured and state the cost thereof, using for such purpose the same formula and basis employed, on the date specified, by the company in calculating single premiums.)

  b Adjustment on account of dividends to credit of policy . . . .
  c **Total** (add lines 56a and 56b). . . . .
  d Outstanding indebtedness against policy . . . .
  e Net total value of policy (for gift or estate tax purposes) (subtract line 56d from line 56c) . . . . .

The undersigned officer of the above-named insurance company hereby certifies that this statement sets forth true and correct information.

Signature ▶	Title ▶	Date of Certification ▶

♲ *Printed on recycled paper* *U.S. Government Printing Office: 1994 — 301-628/00246

9898 ☐ VOID ☐ CORRECTED

PAYER'S name, street address, city, state, and ZIP code	1 Gross distribution $	OMB No. 1545-0119	Distributions From Pensions, Annuities, Retirement or Profit-Sharing Plans, IRAs, Insurance Contracts, etc.
	2a Taxable amount $	**1995** Form **1099-R**	
	2b Taxable amount not determined ☐	Total distribution ☐	**Copy A** **For**
PAYER'S Federal identification number	RECIPIENT'S identification number	3 Capital gain (included in box 2a) $	4 Federal income tax withheld $	**Internal Revenue Service Center** File with Form 1096.
RECIPIENT'S name	5 Employee contributions or insurance premiums $	6 Net unrealized appreciation in employer's securities $	For Paperwork Reduction Act Notice and instructions for completing this form, see **Instructions for Forms 1099, 1098, 5498, and W-2G.**
Street address (including apt. no.)	7 Distribution code	IRA/ SEP ☐	8 Other $ %	
City, state, and ZIP code	9a Your percentage of total distribution %	9b Total employee contributions $	
Account number (optional)	10 State tax withheld $ $	11 State/Payer's state no.	12 State distribution $ $
	13 Local tax withheld $ $	14 Name of locality	15 Local distribution $ $

Form **1099-R**   Cat. No. 14436Q   Department of the Treasury - Internal Revenue Service

Do NOT Cut or Separate Forms on This Page

9898 ☐ VOID ☐ CORRECTED

PAYER'S name, street address, city, state, and ZIP code	1 Gross distribution $	OMB No. 1545-0119	Distributions From Pensions, Annuities, Retirement or Profit-Sharing Plans, IRAs, Insurance Contracts, etc.
	2a Taxable amount $	**1995** Form **1099-R**	
	2b Taxable amount not determined ☐	Total distribution ☐	**Copy A** **For**
PAYER'S Federal identification number	RECIPIENT'S identification number	3 Capital gain (included in box 2a) $	4 Federal income tax withheld $	**Internal Revenue Service Center** File with Form 1096.
RECIPIENT'S name	5 Employee contributions or insurance premiums $	6 Net unrealized appreciation in employer's securities $	For Paperwork Reduction Act Notice and instructions for completing this form, see **Instructions for Forms 1099, 1098, 5498, and W-2G.**
Street address (including apt. no.)	7 Distribution code	IRA/ SEP ☐	8 Other $ %	
City, state, and ZIP code	9a Your percentage of total distribution %	9b Total employee contributions $	
Account number (optional)	10 State tax withheld $ $	11 State/Payer's state no.	12 State distribution $ $
	13 Local tax withheld $ $	14 Name of locality	15 Local distribution $ $

Form **1099-R**   Cat. No. 14436Q   Department of the Treasury - Internal Revenue Service

---

Form 8615

Department of the Treasury
Internal Revenue Service

Tax for Children Under Age 14
Who Have Investment Income of More Than $1,200

▶ See instructions below and on back.
▶ Attach ONLY to the child's Form 1040, Form 1040A, or Form 1040NR.

OMB No. 1545-0998

1994

Attachment
Sequence No. **33**

Child's name shown on return

Child's social security number

A Parent's name (first, initial, and last). **Caution:** See instructions on back before completing.

B Parent's social security number

C Parent's filing status (check one):

☐ Single   ☐ Married filing jointly   ☐ Married filing separately   ☐ Head of household   ☐ Qualifying widow(er)

Step 1   Figure child's net investment income

1	Enter child's investment income, such as taxable interest and dividend income. See instructions. If this amount is $1,200 or less, **stop here;** do not file this form	**1**	
2	If the child DID NOT itemize deductions on Schedule A (Form 1040 or Form 1040NR), enter $1,200. If the child ITEMIZED deductions, see instructions	**2**	
3	Subtract line 2 from line 1. If the result is zero or less, **stop here;** do not complete the rest of this form but ATTACH it to the child's return	**3**	
4	Enter child's **taxable** income from Form 1040, line 37; Form 1040A, line 22; or Form 1040NR, line 36 ▶	**4**	
5	Enter the **smaller** of line 3 or line 4	**5**	

Step 2   Figure tentative tax based on the tax rate of the parent listed on line A

6	Enter parent's **taxable** income from Form 1040, line 37; Form 1040A, line 22; Form 1040EZ, line 5; or Form 1040NR, line 36. If the parent transferred property to a trust, see instructions	**6**	
7	Enter the total net investment income, if any, from Forms 8615, line 5, of ALL OTHER children of the parent identified above. **Do not** include the amount from line 5 above	**7**	
8	Add lines 5, 6, and 7	**8**	
9	Tax on line 8 based on the **parent's** filing status. See instructions. If from Capital Gain Tax Worksheet, enter amount from line 4 of that worksheet here ▶ _____	**9**	
10	Enter parent's tax from Form 1040, line 38; Form 1040A, line 23; Form 1040EZ, line 9; or Form 1040NR, line 37. If from **Capital Gain Tax Worksheet,** enter amount from line 4 of that worksheet here ▶ _____	**10**	
11	Subtract line 10 from line 9. If line 7 is blank, enter on line 13 the amount from line 11; skip lines 12a and 12b	**11**	
12a	Add lines 5 and 7	**12a**	
b	Divide line 5 by line 12a. Enter the result as a decimal (rounded to two places)	**12b**	×
13	Multiply line 11 by line 12b	**13**	

Step 3   Figure child's tax—If lines 4 and 5 above are the same, enter -0- on line 15 and go to line 16.

14	Subtract line 5 from line 4	**14**	
15	Tax on line 14 based on the **child's** filing status. See instructions. If from Capital Gain Tax Worksheet, enter amount from line 4 of that worksheet here ▶ _____	**15**	
16	Add lines 13 and 15	**16**	
17	Tax on line 4 based on the **child's** filing status. See instructions. If from Capital Gain Tax Worksheet, check here ▶ ☐	**17**	
18	Enter the **larger** of line 16 or line 17 here and on Form 1040, line 38; Form 1040A, line 23; or Form 1040NR, line 37. Be sure to check the box for "Form 8615" even if line 17 is more than line 16 ▶	**18**	

General Instructions

Purpose of Form.—For children under age 14, investment income over $1,200 is taxed at the parent's rate if the parent's rate is higher than the child's rate. If the child's investment income is more than $1,200, use this form to figure the child's tax.

Investment Income.—As used on this form, "investment income" includes all taxable income other than earned income as defined on page 2. It includes income such as taxable interest, dividends, capital gains, rents, royalties, etc. It also includes pension and annuity

income and income (other than earned income) received as the beneficiary of a trust.

Who Must File.—Generally, Form 8615 must be filed for any child who was under age 14 on January 1, 1995, had more than $1,200 of investment income, and is required to file a tax return. If neither parent was alive on December 31, 1994, do not use Form 8615. Instead, figure the child's tax in the normal manner.

Note: The parent may be able to elect to report the child's interest and dividends on his or her return. If the parent makes this election, the child will not have to

file a return or Form 8615. For more details, see the instructions for Form 1040 or Form 1040A, or get **Form 8814,** Parents' Election To Report Child's Interest and Dividends.

Additional Information.—For more details, get **Pub. 929,** Tax Rules for Children and Dependents.

Incomplete Information for Parent.—If the parent's taxable income or filing status or the net investment income of the parent's other children is not known by the due date of the child's return, reasonable estimates may be used. Write "Estimated" on the appropriate line(s) of Form 8615. For more details, see Pub. 929.

For Paperwork Reduction Act Notice, see back of form.   Cat. No. 64113U   Form **8615** (1994)

Appendix C
Texas Directive
to Physicians

TEXAS
DIRECTIVE TO PHYSICIANS

Directive made this _____ day of _____.

(day)   (month, year)

I, _____,

(name)

being of sound mind, wilfully and voluntarily make known my desire that my life shall not be artificially prolonged under the circumstances set forth in this directive.

1. If at any time I should have an incurable or irreversible condition caused by injury, disease, or illness certified to be a terminal condition by two physicians, and if the application of life-sustaining procedures would serve only to artificially postpone the moment of my death, and if my attending physician determines that my death is imminent or will result within a relatively short time without the application of life-sustaining procedures, I direct that those procedures be withheld or withdrawn, and that I be permitted to die naturally.

2. In the absence of my ability to give directions regarding the use of those life-sustaining procedures, it is my intention that this directive be honored by my family and physicians as the final expression of my legal right to refuse medical or surgical treatment and accept the consequences from such refusal.

Other directions:

3. If I have been diagnosed as pregnant and that diagnosis is known to my physician, this directive has no effect during my pregnancy.

4. This directive is in effect until it is revoked.

5. I understand the full import of this directive and I am emotionally and mentally competent to make this directive.

6. I understand that I may revoke this directive at any time.

SIGN THE DOCUMENT AND PRINT YOUR CITY, COUNTY AND STATE OF RESIDENCE

Signed _____

City, County and State of Residence _____

WITNESSING PROCEDURE

TWO WITNESSES MUST SIGN BELOW

I am not related to the declarant by blood or marriage. I would not be entitled to any portion of the declarant's estate on the declarant's death. I am not the attending physician of the declarant or an employee of the attending physician. I am not a patient in the health care facility in which the declarant is a patient. I have no claim against any portion of the declarant's estate on the declarant's death. Furthermore, if I am an employee of a health facility in which the declarant is a patient, I am not involved in providing direct patient care to the declarant and I am not directly involved in the financial affairs of the health facility.

WITNESS #1   Witness _____

WITNESS #2   Witness _____

Courtesy of *Choice In Dying*
200 Varick Street, New York, NY 10014 (212) 366-5540

11/95

Appendix D
Texas Durable Power of Attorney for Health Care

TEXAS DURABLE POWER OF ATTORNEY FOR HEALTH CARE

INFORMATION CONCERNING THE DURABLE POWER OF ATTORNEY FOR HEALTH CARE

THIS IS AN IMPORTANT LEGAL DOCUMENT. BEFORE SIGNING THIS DOCUMENT, YOU SHOULD KNOW THESE IMPORTANT FACTS:

Except to the extent you state otherwise, this document gives the person you name as your agent the authority to make any and all health care decisions for you in accordance with your wishes, including your religious and moral beliefs, when you are no longer capable of making them yourself. Because "health care" means any treatment, service, or procedure to maintain, diagnose, or treat your physical or mental condition, your agent has the power to make a broad range of health care decisions for you. Your agent may consent, refuse to consent, or withdraw consent to medical treatment and may make decisions about withdrawing or withholding life-sustaining treatment. Your agent may not consent to voluntary inpatient mental health services, convulsive treatment, psychosurgery, or abortion. A physician must comply with your agent's instructions or allow you to be transferred to another physician.

Your agent's authority begins when your doctor certifies that you lack the capacity to make health care decisions.

Your agent is obligated to follow your instructions when making decisions on your behalf. Unless you state otherwise, your agent has the same authority to make decisions about your health care as you would have had.

It is important that you discuss this document with your physician or other health care provider before you sign it to make sure that you understand the nature and range of decisions that may be made on your behalf. If you do not have a physician, you should talk with someone else who is knowledgeable about these issues and can answer your questions. You do not need a lawyer's assistance to complete this document, but if there is anything in this document that you do not understand, you should ask a lawyer to explain it to you.

The person you appoint as agent should be someone you know and trust. The person must be 18 years of age or older or a person under 18 years of age who has had the disabilities of minority removed. If you appoint your health or residential care provider (e.g., your physician or an employee of a home health agency, hospital, nursing home, or residential care home, other than a relative), that person has to choose between acting as your agent or as your health or residential care provider; the law does not permit a person to do both at the same time.

You should inform the person you appoint that you want the person to be your health care agent. You should discuss this document with your agent and your physician and give each a signed copy.

You should indicate on the document itself the people and institutions who have signed copies. Your agent is not liable for health care decisions made in good faith on your behalf.

Even after you have signed this document, you have the right to make health care decisions for yourself as long as you are able to do so and treatment cannot be given to you or stopped over your objection. You have the right to revoke the authority granted to your agent by informing your agent or your health or residential care provider orally or in writing, or by your execution of a subsequent durable power of attorney for health care. Unless you state otherwise, your appointment of a spouse dissolves on divorce.

This document may not be changed or modified. If you want to make changes in the document, you must make an entirely new one.

You may wish to designate an alternate agent in the event that your agent is unwilling, unable, or ineligible to act as your agent. Any alternate agent you designate has the same authority to make health care decisions for you.

THIS POWER OF ATTORNEY IS NOT VALID UNLESS IT IS SIGNED IN THE PRESENCE OF TWO OR MORE QUALIFIED WITNESSES. THE FOLLOWING PERSONS MAY NOT ACT AS WITNESSES:

(1) the person you have designated as your agent;

(2) your health or residential care provider or an employee of your health or residential care provider;

(3) your spouse;

(4) your lawful heirs or beneficiaries named in your will or a deed; or

(5) creditors or persons who have a claim against you.

TEXAS DURABLE POWER OF ATTORNEY FOR HEALTH CARE

INSTRUCTIONS

PRINT YOUR NAME

PRINT THE NAME, ADDRESS AND HOME AND WORK TELEPHONE NUMBERS OF YOUR AGENT

STATE LIMITATIONS ON YOUR AGENT'S POWER (IF ANY)

DESIGNATION OF HEALTH CARE AGENT.

I, _____, appoint:
(name)

_____
(name of agent)

_____
(address)

_____
(work telephone number)   *(home telephone number)*

as my agent to make any and all health care decisions for me, except to the extent I state otherwise in this document. This durable power of attorney for health care takes effect if I become unable to make my own health care decisions and this fact is certified in writing by my physician.

LIMITATIONS ON THE DECISION MAKING AUTHORITY OF MY AGENT ARE AS FOLLOWS.

© 1995
CHOICE IN DYING, INC.

PRINT THE NAME, ADDRESS AND HOME AND WORK TELEPHONE NUMBERS OF YOUR FIRST AND SECOND ALTERNATE AGENTS

DESIGNATION OF ALTERNATE AGENT.

(You are not required to designate an alternate agent but you may do so. An alternate agent may make the same health care decisions as the designated agent if the designated agent is unable or unwilling to act as your agent. If the agent designated is your spouse, the designation is automatically revoked by law if your marriage is dissolved.)

If the person designated as my agent is unable or unwilling to make health care decisions for me, I designate the following persons to serve as my agent to make health care decisions for me as authorized by this document, who serve in the following order:

FIRST ALTERNATE

A. First Alternate Agent

_____
(name of first alternate agent)

_____
(home address)

_____
(work telephone number)   *(home telephone number)*

SECOND ALTERNATE

B. Second Alternate Agent

_____
(name of second alternate agent)

_____
(home address)

_____
(work telephone number)   *(home telephone number)*

LOCATION OF ORIGINAL

The original of this document is kept at: _____

_____

© 1995
CHOICE IN DYING, INC.

LOCATION OF COPIES

The following individuals or institutions have signed copies:

Name: _____

Address: _____

Name: _____

Address: _____

DURATION.

I understand that this power of attorney exists indefinitely from the date I execute this document unless I establish a shorter time or revoke the power of attorney. If I am unable to make health care decisions for myself when this power of attorney expires, the authority I have granted my agent continues to exist until the time I become able to make health care decisions for myself.

EXPIRATION DATE (IF ANY)

(IF APPLICABLE) This power of attorney ends on the following date:

_____

PRIOR DESIGNATIONS REVOKED.

I revoke any prior power of attorney for health care.

ACKNOWLEDGMENT OF DISCLOSURE STATEMENT.

I have been provided with a disclosure statement explaining the effect of this document. I have read and understood that information contained in the disclosure statement.

(YOU MUST DATE AND SIGN THIS POWER OF ATTORNEY)

PRINT THE DATE

I sign my name to this durable power of attorney for health care on _____
(date)

PRINT YOUR LOCATION

day of _____ 19_____, at _____.
       (month)   *(city and state)*

SIGN THE DOCUMENT

_____
(signature)

PRINT YOUR NAME

_____
(print name)

© 1995
CHOICE IN DYING, INC.

WITNESSING PROCEDURE

YOUR TWO WITNESSES MUST SIGN AND DATE YOUR DOCUMENT BELOW

THEY MUST ALSO PRINT THEIR NAMES AND ADDRESSES

STATEMENT OF WITNESSES.

I declare under penalty of perjury that the principal has identified himself or herself to me, that the principal signed or acknowledged this durable power of attorney in my presence, that I believe the principal to be of sound mind, that the principal has affirmed that the principal is aware of the nature of the document and is signing it voluntarily and free from duress, that the principal requested that I serve as witness to the principal's execution of this document, that I am not the person appointed as agent by this document, and that I am not a provider of health or residential care, an employee of a provider of health or residential care, the operator of a community care facility, or an employee of an operator of a health care facility.

I declare that I am not related to the principal by blood, marriage, or adoption and that to the best of my knowledge I am not entitled to any part of the estate of the principal on the death of the principal under a will or by operation of law.

WITNESS #1

Witness Signature: _____

Print Name: _____ Date: _____

Address: _____

WITNESS #2

Witness Signature: _____

Print Name: _____ Date: _____

Address: _____

Courtesy of *Choice In Dying*
200 Varick Street, New York, NY 10014 (212) 366-5540

11/95

Glossary

Estate planning has its own vocabulary. Therefore, you might be unfamiliar with many of the terms and words in this book. This glossary will help you understand and use them.

administrator A person appointed by the probate court to administer the estate of someone who has died without a will. An administrator plays the same role as an executor.

beneficiary A charitable organization, another nonprofit group or a person who receives money or other property from a will, trust, custodial account, etc.

bequest A gift of personal property in a will, such as jewelry, furniture, clothes or a car. For purposes of estate planning, personal property is distinguished from real property. You cannot make a bequest of real property, which includes homes, other buildings and land.

bond A document promising that if a person in a position of responsibility—such as an executor, a custodian or a trustee—fails to carry out his or her duties in the best interest of an individual's family or other beneficiaries, anyone damaged by the failure will be paid a certain amount of money by a bonding or an insurance company.

codicil An amendment to a will. Generally, codicils are used to make relatively simple changes to a will. They are con-

sidered part of a will and must meet the same legal requirements as a will.

community property Property acquired by a couple during their marriage and owned jointly by both spouses. Each has a legal claim to half of all community property. Nine states—Arizona, California, Idaho, Louisiana, Nevada, New Mexico, Texas, Washington and Wisconsin—are community property states. The others are separate property states.

custodian The person named to manage assets placed in a custodial account set up under either the Uniform Gifts to Minors Act or the Uniform Transfers to Minors Act.

death taxes A general term for estate and inheritance taxes.

devise A gift of personal or real property made under a will.

disinheritance Excluding a family member from a will.

equity The difference between the current market value of an asset and what is owed on it.

estate All of the property a person owns at the time of his or her death. Property conveyed to others through a will is considered a probate estate and will go through the probate process.

estate planning The process of planning for the disposal of assets upon death; protecting an estate from creditor actions; minimizing estate taxes; minimizing the number of assets that will go through probate; planning for the possibility of mental or physical incapacitation; and preparing health care directives.

executor The person named in a will to administer that estate after the owner dies. The executor makes sure that the terms of the will are carried out.

gift The transfer of an interest in a piece of property from one person to another without consideration. The property can include money, stocks, bonds and real estate, for example.

gift tax A tax on completed transfers of property without consideration exceeding a certain amount.

heir A person entitled by the laws of a state to inherit property from an estate if no will exists.

holographic will A handwritten will, invalid in most states.

inheritance tax A tax paid by the beneficiaries of an estate.

***inter vivos* trust** A revocable or irrevocable trust that is created, or set up, while the settlor is still alive; sometimes referred to as a living trust.

intestate Having made no legal will.

irrevocable trust A trust that cannot be changed after it is established.

joint tenancy A type of property ownership that allows two or more persons to own an asset. If one of the owners dies, the other owner(s) automatically own(s) the deceased's share. This is a common form of ownership for married couples and unmarried couples in committed relationships.

joint will A single will signed by two spouses.

legacy A transfer of personal property through a will.

living trust A type of trust set up while the settlor is still alive. It can be irrevocable but is generally revocable, which means that it can be changed or revoked. See *inter vivos* trust.

living will A document indicating under what conditions the undersigned want to be kept alive by artificial means if he or she is critically ill or injured.

marital deduction A federal tax deduction that allows one spouse to pass on to the other his or her entire estate tax free, regardless of its worth.

minor child Depending on the state, a child who is younger than 18 or 21 years of age.

personal property Everything owned other than real property, which includes buildings and land.

probate A legal process that proves the validity of a will, pays an estate's debts and taxes and distributes its property to the beneficiaries according to the terms of the will.

probate estate The property owned that passes to others under a will and through probate.

real property Real estate—homes, other buildings and land.

residuary beneficiary The beneficiary named in a will who receives anything in the estate not specifically designated to another beneficiary after all claims against the estate, including taxes, are paid.

revocable trust A trust that can be changed or revoked while its settlor is alive.

settlor The formal term for someone who creates a trust; also called a trustor, grantor or donor.

taking against a will An option given to a surviving spouse in a separate property state to inherit what he or she is legally entitled to receive from the deceased's estate according to state laws rather than what he or she was left in the deceased's will.

taxable estate The value of an estate that is subject to federal and state taxes after the owner's death.

tenancy by the entirety A form of joint ownership available only to spouses and only in certain states.

tenants in common A type of property ownership that gives each owner a share of an asset without an interest in the other's share or rights of survivorship.

testamentary trust A type of trust that is part of a will and that is not actually created until the testator dies. This kind of will is always irrevocable.

testator The person who writes a will.

trust A legal entity that can be created to hold and manage property for one or more beneficiaries. The trust property is managed and distributed by a trustee who holds legal title to the trust property. The trust beneficiary(ies) take(s) control of the property at a time specified in the document creating the trust.

trustee The person who manages the assets in a trust.

Uniform Gifts to Minors Act or Uniform Transfers to Minors Act A law that allows a person to establish a custodial account on behalf of a minor child and place certain types of assets in the account. A custodian manages the assets until the minor reaches age 18 or 21 in most states. Some version of this law is valid in all states.

will A legal document that spells out whom the testator wants to receive certain property the testator owns after he or she dies. If the testator is the parent of a minor child, the testator can also use the will to designate personal and property guardians for the child.

Index